ESSENTIAL
SEWING GUIDE

NANCY ZIEMAN

Oxmoor House®

ESSENTIAL SEWING GUIDE

by Nancy Zieman

from the "Sewing with Nancy" series

©1998 by Nancy Zieman and Oxmoor House, Inc.

Book Division of Southern Progress Corporation

P.O. Box 2463, Birmingham, Alabama 35201

Published by Oxmoor House, Inc., and Leisure Arts, Inc.

Library of Congress Catalog Number: 98-65199

Hardcover ISBN: 0-8487-1680-9

Softcover ISBN: 0-8487-1681-7

Manufactured in the United States of America

First Printing 1998

Editor-in-Chief: Nancy Fitzpatrick Wyatt

Senior Crafts Editor: Susan Ramey Cleveland

Senior Editor, Editorial Services: Olivia Kindig Wells

Art Director: James Boone

ESSENTIAL SEWING GUIDE

Editor: Lois Martin

Editorial Assistant: Cecile Y. Nierodzinski

Copy Editor: Anne S. Dickson

Proofreader: Catherine S. Ritter

Associate Art Director: Cynthia R. Cooper

Designer: Rita Yerby

Production Director: Phillip Lee

Associate Production Manager: Theresa L. Beste

Senior Photographer: John O'Hagan

Photographer: Brit Huckabay

Photo Stylists: Virginia R. Cravens, Catherine A. Pittman

Illustrator: Rochelle Stibb

Editorial Assistance, Nancy's Notions: Betty Hanneman

We're Here for You!

We at Oxmoor House are dedicated to serving you with reliable information that expands your imagination and enriches your life. We welcome your comments and suggestions. Please write us at:

Oxmoor House, Inc.
Editor, *Essential Sewing Guide*
2100 Lakeshore Drive
Birmingham, AL 35209

To order additional publications, call 1-205-877-6560.

The editor thanks Mark McDowell and the staff of the Sewing Machine Mart in Homewood, Alabama, for lending the Pfaff sewing machines and sergers used in photography.

Have you ever left a beautiful piece of fabric in the store because you weren't sure how to handle it? Does it seem to take you a long time to insert a zipper correctly? Have you put off buying a serger or a new sewing machine because you aren't sure what to look for? • **No matter how long we've been sewing,** we can always come up with a question about a tool or a technique. It may be something we've never tried before, or it may just be something we've forgotten. • **I think this book can help you,** no matter what your sewing level. You can find very basic information, such as how to stitch a straight seam and how to tie a good knot for hand sewing. You can also learn advanced techniques, such as stitching a double welt pocket in a jacket and adjusting a skirt pattern so that the zipper extends to the top of the waistband. Use the charts in the back for quick reference on everything from the best needle to the right pattern size. • **Share your love of sewing!** Use what you already know and what you learn from this book to teach someone else to sew. Join a sewing group. Organize a volunteer project to sew for charity. You'll find it's "sew" rewarding.

Nancy Zieman

CONTENTS

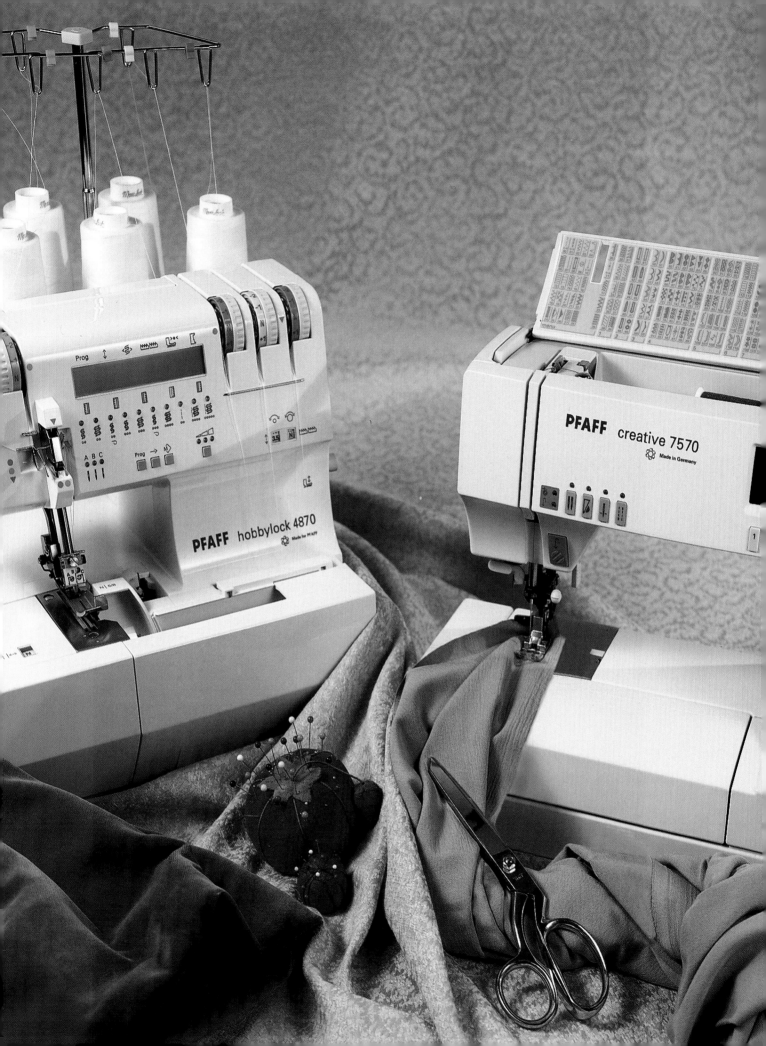

EQUIPMENT

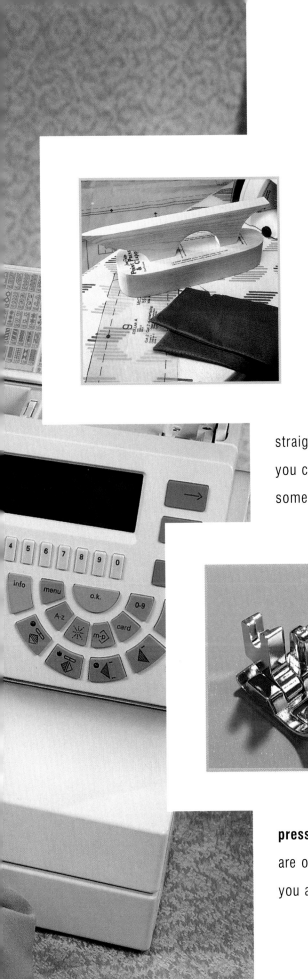

Having an entire room devoted to sewing is a luxury many of us wish for. Often, our sewing space is a corner of a bedroom, the family room, or another part of the house. Many of us must store our sewing equipment and supplies, bringing them out only when we're working on projects. But no matter how big or permanent your sewing "room" is, you need some basic equipment for it. • **A basic sewing machine** that has a straightstitch and a zigzag stitch will serve you for most projects. But you can also have a lot of fun using the special features available on some of the medium-priced and top-of-the-line machines—plus they make routine tasks like sewing button-holes much easier and faster. Add the right presser feet and you'll be amazed at how quick and simple even complex projects become. • **Home sergers are gaining favor** among sewers. Sergers stitch, finish, and trim seams all at the same time. You can use two, three, four, or even five threads to create special overlock and flatlock stitches, as well as other decorative stitches. • **The right pressing equipment is essential.** A good iron and a sturdy ironing board are only the beginning. If you want to sew beautifully made garments, you also need the right pressing accessories to build in shape.

YOUR SEWING space

Whether you sew on your kitchen table or in a special sewing room, you need a few basics.

Work Surfaces

Choose a sturdy work table large enough to lay out and cut your projects. This table should be high enough so that you're comfortable working at it while standing up. If you need to raise your table, put an industrial-size can under each leg, or cut lengths of PVC (plastic) pipe and place the legs in them. Just be sure that your table is secure and won't fall off the cans or slip through the pipes.

Pad the table to avoid cutting or marking its surface. Use a cutting mat or a dining table pad, or make a pad from an old blanket.

Make sure that the table for your machines is the right height for you to sit and sew without causing back strain. This table should be sturdy enough to absorb vibrations from your machine.

Lighting

Sewing machines have built-in lights to illuminate the sewing surface. But you also need good task lighting in the room. Overhead light can cast shadows as you bend over the work surface to lay out a garment. Choose a good desk lamp or other task lighting for each part of your sewing space.

Pressing Center

One key to giving your garments or projects a professional look is to press as you sew. Your sewing area should include a place for your iron and ironing board and other pressing equipment and notions.

> ### Note from Nancy
>
> *While I'm sewing, I lower my ironing board to the same height as my sewing table and place it right next to me. That way I can press each seam as I finish it without having to get up each time.*

Seating

Choose an adjustable chair with good back support in order to prevent back strain as you sew. If your chair has wheels, you can move easily from sewing machine to pressing center to serger.

Supplies

Keep on hand a stock of basic supplies, such as interfacing, thread, zippers, and buttons. Doing so eliminates time-consuming trips to the store and makes it easy to complete quick repair jobs.

The most productive seamstresses I know always have other basic notions—elastics, linings, snaps, and hooks and eyes—on hand, too. Stick with basic colors or your favorite accent colors (or shades that blend with them).

You also need good scissors, replacement needles and serger blades for your machines, pins, fabric markers or chalk, a tape measure, and a ruler. Throughout this book, you'll also find notions that can help simplify or speed your sewing (or both!). See page 147 for a list of sewing notions.

Storage

If you use your sewing space for other activities, you need storage space for equipment as well as for fabric, supplies, and notions. Always store fabric and thread away from light (which can cause fading). Protect all stored items from dust.

By organizing your sewing projects before you store them, you save time when you're ready to start or continue a project. When you buy fabric for a specific project, check the back of the pattern envelope for recommended notions, and make sure you have them all. When you get home, put together everything you need for the project—fabric, interfacing, thread, zipper, and other notions—before you store them. Try one of these tried-and-true storage methods:

• **Wrap smaller project ingredients inside the fabric**, and place the fabric on a shelf or in a drawer near your sewing area. Put the easiest-to-misplace items, such as buttons, in a regular envelope.

• **Enclose all items in a large bag**. Clear plastic works best because you can see the contents.

• **Store fabric, notions, and findings in an inexpensive plastic storage basket or bin** (sold at discount and variety stores). This is my favorite method. It's also the method we use in the dressmaking department at Nancy's Notions.

machines

Today's sewing machines come in many varieties and price ranges. You can buy a simple, mechanical-action machine that offers nothing more than straightstitching and zigzagging. Or you can choose a top-of-the-line computerized machine that creates custom embroidery, figures patchwork quilting yardages, and offers other special features.

Choosing a Sewing Machine

You can sew virtually any project using the most basic sewing machine, but you may need more time and skill than you would with a machine that offers more features. For example, you can make buttonholes on a basic machine, but using a machine with a buttonhole feature greatly simplifies the task. If you have a basic machine, you must sew some types of stitches (such as decorative embroidery stitches) by hand. I recommend that you buy the most versatile machine you can afford. Consider the following tips when you shop for a sewing machine:

• **Know what kind of sewing most interests you.** If you're primarily interested in making draperies and other home decor items, you may not care how easy it is to use a machine's buttonhole feature. If you're a quilter, the machine features that appeal to you will be very different from what a machine embroiderer will want.

• **Talk to your dealer about the features you want, and try out**

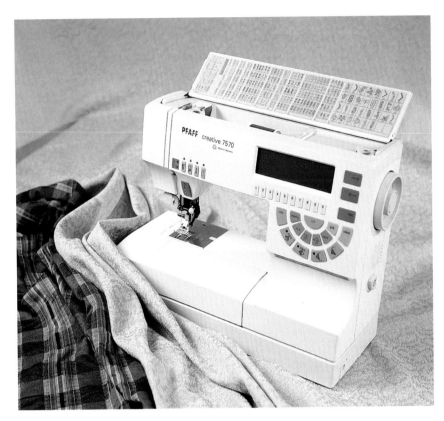

several machines. If you know that you'll be sewing on a particular type of fabric (heavy drapery fabrics, slippery silks, or cotton quilting fabrics, for example), take samples with you and try out machines using those types of fabric. If the dealer offers classes, sign up for one to get a feel for how a machine works.

• **Find out what kind of support the dealer and the manufacturer offer.** Does the machine come with a workbook or a video that explains how to use it? Does the dealer offer classes? Is service available? What sort of warranty does the manufacturer offer on the machine?

Sewing Machine Types

Sewing machines are almost as varied as the people who use them. You can spend a few hundred dollars for a basic machine or invest thousands of dollars in top-of-the-line equipment and accessories. I've divided sewing machines into three categories: basic, medium-priced, and top-of-the-line. When you shop for a sewing machine, look for these key features:

• **A basic sewing machine** should have the capacity to make straight stitches and to sew zigzag stitches in several widths. You can find a basic machine with anywhere from five stitches to almost two dozen stitches. In addition to the straight and zigzag stitches, look for a feature that lets you make a buttonhole without turning your fabric. A blindhem stitch and one or more stitches designed especially for sewing knits ("stretch" stitches) are also useful.

Make sure that it's easy to adjust the stitch length and the upper thread tension. Bobbin tension is preset, but check how easy it is to wind and load the bobbin. Unless you're buying a portable machine, look for easy conversion from a flatbed sewing surface to a free-arm surface (for stitching armholes, cuffs, and other small areas).

Almost all sewing machines have a sewing light and a thread cutter.

• **Medium-priced machines** offer all the same features as basic machines, but they include more stitches—sometimes as many as 60 or 70. Most of these additional stitches are decorative. Even if you don't plan to do machine embroidery, you'll find that a decorative stitch makes an attractive alternative to plain topstitching.

Medium-priced machines may be mechanical or computerized. The computerized models may offer ways to customize embroidery stitches or patterns. Features to look for include a self-threading needle, adjustable needle positions, and handy built-in storage for sewing accessories. If the machine is computerized, consider the size and readability of the message screen.

• **Top-of-the-line machines** are almost always computerized. Some of them allow you to connect the

machine to your home computer so that you can stitch custom embroidery designs, figure patchwork quilting yardages, and complete other tasks.

Many of the newer top-of-the-line models provide embroidery stitches and designs on computer cards. This feature allows you to add to your choice of stitches and embroidery patterns almost indefinitely. Some companies sell scanners that allow you to create embroidery designs from any visual image you choose. These machines usually come with anywhere from 100 to 500 stitches programmed into the machine.

Most top-of-the-line machines monitor your bobbin thread and let you know when it's low. Many models feature the ability to use two thread colors at once, dual feed (to ease sewing thick or slippery fabrics), and a built-in instruction manual. Others offer special features for quilters, such as a stitch designed to simulate hand quilting and the ability to program a specific stitch length into the machine.

• Some manufacturers offer **accessory machines.** If you have a basic or medium-priced machine that you're happy with for regular sewing, you can buy an accessory machine that has top-of-the-line machine stitches and functions without trading in your sewing machine. These include personal embroidery machines and blind-hemming machines.

Using the Manual

Your owner's manual is a great resource for learning how to thread and adjust the machine, plus how to wind and thread the bobbin. Each manufacturer has its own style for these basic tasks. Your manual also offers troubleshooting tips to help if you have problems with stitches or the machine's operation. Most manuals contain a list of accessories available from the manufacturer, such as special presser feet, cleaning equipment, and replacement parts.

Note from Nancy

I personalized my owner's manual by putting Post-It Notes on pages I refer to often. It's amazing how many times I go back to certain pages; the markers speed up this process.

Buying a Used Machine

Most dealers take trade-ins when you buy a new sewing machine, and then they sell these second-hand machines. You can find a used machine through newspaper ads, at yard sales, or at estate sales.

Buying a used machine is much like buying a new one. You should know what kind of sewing you plan to do, and the machine should have all the features you need. Try out the machine to be sure it's easy to use and that it's in proper working order.

If the seller no longer has the owner's manual, buy a replacement manual from a dealer or from the manufacturer. You may want to take the machine to a dealer for cleaning and servicing, especially if it hasn't been used in a while. Ask the dealer if replacement parts are still available.

Identifying Sewing Machine Parts

The *Diagram* (right) shows a generic sewing machine. Your machine may look different, but it has the same major parts. Check your owner's manual if you can't match parts of this diagram with your machine.

- **Balance wheel** (also called the handwheel or flywheel) makes a complete turn with each stitch.
- **Bobbin** holds the lower thread supply.
- **Bobbin winder** holds the bobbin while you wind thread onto it.
- **Feed dogs** hold the fabric tight against the presser foot as stitches are formed and move back and forth to feed (or advance) the fabric through the machine.
- **Foot control** is the "gas pedal" that controls how fast or slow the machine sews.
- **Presser foot** holds the fabric against the throat plate during sewing.
- **Presser foot lever** or lifter raises and lowers the presser foot. This lever must be lowered when you sew, or threads will knot and jam the machine.
- **Spool pin** holds the thread spool.
- **Stitch length regulator** determines the length of each stitch. For general sewing, set the stitch length at 10 to 12 stitches per inch. On some machines, this setting is marked 2.5.
- **Stitch width regulator** deter-

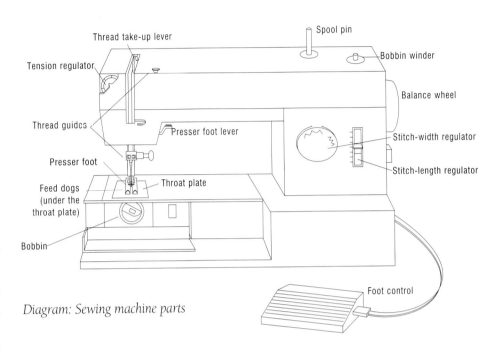

Diagram: Sewing machine parts

mines the width of a zigzag stitch.
- **Tension regulator** controls the tightness of the upper thread. See your owner's manual for settings.
- **Thread guides** hold the thread as it moves from the spool to the needle. The number and location of these guides varies.
- **Thread take-up lever** moves up and down with the needle, taking up thread slack with each stitch.
- **Throat plate** is a metal piece on the base or bed of the machine, under the presser foot. It contains the opening for the feed dogs and the needle, plus marks for seam widths.

Maintaining Your Machine

Sewing machines are sturdy pieces of equipment, so a little regular maintenance goes a long way to keeping your machine in good working order. Cleaning and oiling

your machine before each project reduces the likelihood of mechanical problems while you're sewing.
- Insert a new needle for each project. Don't wait for a needle to break or start snagging your fabric. A worn needle can develop tiny burrs and other imperfections that will cause your machine to skip stitches or make uneven stitches.
- Whenever you change the top thread, "floss" your machine by clipping the thread at the spool and pulling the thread out through the needle. This helps remove built-up lint.
- Remove the bobbin case, which holds the lower thread, and dust or wipe it out to remove lint. Refer to the owner's manual and, if it's recommended, place a drop of oil at the machine hook.

serger

The serger is to sewing what the microwave oven is to cooking. A serger lets you complete some sewing tasks in much less time than the same tasks would take on a conventional sewing machine.

Simply stated, a serger stitches a seam, trims the excess fabric, and finishes the raw edges, all in one step. And it does this nearly twice as fast as a conventional sewing machine can stitch a seam. Also called overlock machines, sergers have been used by the ready-to-wear industry for years.

Just as microwave ovens haven't replaced conventional ovens in most kitchens, a serger won't replace your sewing machine. Sergers are accessory machines that help you enhance speed, neatness, and creative possibilities. Because of the serger's unique method of stitching, industry innovators have developed new serger threads, timesaving notions, and creative techniques specifically for use with these machines.

Sergers are generally described by the number of threads the machine uses, such as "3-thread," "3/4-thread," "4/2-thread," or "5-thread" serger. Some models can be converted to produce additional stitches; for instance, some 3/4- and 5-thread machines have 2-thread capability.

Choosing a Serger

When you shop for a serger, follow the same basic guidelines for buying a conventional sewing machine (see page 9).

• **Know how you plan to use the serger.** Will you use it for finishing seams, decorative techniques, home decor, garments, or all-purpose serging? Usually, the more types of stitches a serger can do, the more complex it is to operate.
• **Talk to your dealer** and try out the machine.
• **Check out the kind of support your dealer offers.**

Types of Sergers

Just as sewing machines are sold with different features in different price ranges, sergers also come in three basic levels.
• **A basic serger** should have the capacity to stitch with at least three threads. A 3/4-thread machine is a good choice because it gives you many stitch options. You can buy a 2-thread, single-needle serger, but this basic machine doesn't offer many stitches. A 2-thread machine doesn't make a basic serger stitch, the true overlock stitch.

Adjusting the serger's tension, stitch length, and stitch width should be easy. Some of the basic machines have waste containers attached to catch fabric the machine trims away. They may also have automatic thread cutters. Be sure your serger uses standard machine needles rather than the more heavy-duty industrial serger needles (or be sure you have a convenient source for the industrial needles).
• **A medium-priced serger** has all the features of a basic serger plus more. Some models have a built-in

rolled-edge setting, a popular serged stitch that rolls fabric edges under, providing a neat, attractive finish. Some allow you to disengage the knife to keep you from cutting elastic or ribbon while serging them to a project. Others include self-threading loopers to simplify the task of threading a serger.

• **A top-of-the-line serger** has the capacity to use at least four and possibly five threads. It often has "differential feed," an adjustment knob or lever to control how taut the feed dogs hold fabric being serged; this feature makes it easier to stitch knits and fine or sheer fabrics.

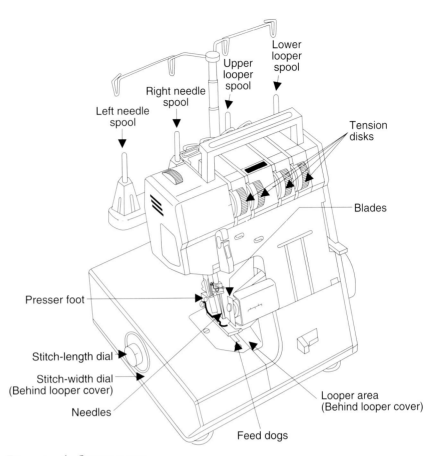

Diagram A: Serger parts

Using the Manual

As with your sewing machine manual, the serger owner's manual shows you how to thread and adjust the machine and informs you about other basic operating techniques. The manual should include troubleshooting tips to help if you have particular problems with stitches

or the serger's operation. It should also provide a list of accessories available from the manufacturer.

Identifying Serger Parts

If serger terminology is new to you, the diagrams and brief definitions in this section will help you understand this new sewing language. *Diagram A* shows a generic 3/4-thread serger; the exact placement of various parts may be different on your model. If you can't identify a part from the diagram, refer to your owner's manual.

• **Loopers** are the serger's "bobbins;" they loop the threads together in a knitlike fashion (*Diagram B*).

• **Upper looper thread** is the second (on a 3-thread serger) or third (on a 3/4- or 5-thread serger) thread from the right. This thread

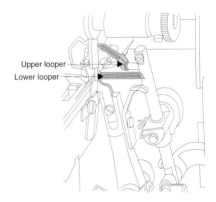

Diagram B: Loopers

does not pass through the fabric; instead, it passes over the surface of the fabric, catching the needle thread on the left and the lower looper thread on the right.

• **Lower looper thread** is the last thread cone on the right on all but 5-thread sergers (where it's fourth from the right). Like the upper looper, the lower looper thread doesn't pass through the fabric; instead, it passes underneath the fabric, catching the needle thread on the left and the upper looper thread on the right.

• **Feed dogs** are teethlike grippers nestled in the serger throat plate that pull the fabric through the machine under the needles. Serger feed dogs are nearly twice as long as those on a sewing machine.

• **Presser foot** holds the fabric taut against the throat plate during serging. You seldom need to raise the presser foot when beginning to serge. Simply lay the fabric on the machine in front of the presser foot and sew; the fabric feeds evenly under the foot. Serger feet are longer than conventional sewing machine feet, and most of them have a "stitch finger" over which stitches form (*Diagram*). Two standard feet are usually included with your serger. One has a wider stitch finger for basic overlock seaming; the other has a narrower stitch finger for rolled-edge (or narrow-edge) serging.

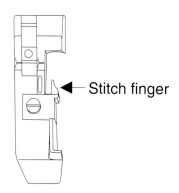

Diagram: Stitch finger

• **Blades** (also called knives) trim seam allowances as you serge. One blade remains stationary while the other moves up and down with the needle. This mouthlike configuration lets the blades "bite" the fabric as you stitch, trimming seam allowances to ¼".

Note from Nancy

Remember that the fabric is cut before it's serged, so you must guide fabric accurately under the foot. You cannot make any adjustments at the needle. Also, for neat, even cutting, make sure the fabric layers fit in the mouthlike opening of the blades.

• **Tension disks** or dials, one for each thread, allow you to adjust the tensions when changing fabrics, stitches, or thread.

• **Stitch-length dial** determines the spacing of the stitches. Stitch length on most sergers ranges from 0.5 mm to 5 mm (from fine satin serging to about 4 or 5 stitches per inch).

• **Stitch-width dial** adjusts the stitch width—the distance between the needle and the blades. This distance is referred to as the "bite." As with other serger measurements, the width is given in millimeters: 0.5 mm to 5 mm (from very narrow to about ³⁄₁₆" or ¼"), with some sergers capable of stitch widths as wide as 7.5 mm (³⁄₈").

• **Needle** requirements vary among machines. Most sergers use regular sewing machine needles, which have shanks with one flat side. But some machines use industrial overlock needles with a round shank. These may be harder to find than sewing machine needles. Check your manual to be sure what type of needle your serger uses.

Although basic 2- and 3-thread sergers have one needle, models with 4- or 5-thread capability have two needles. On these machines, you can use one or both needles, depending on the width and type of stitch desired.

Maintaining Your Serger

Perform routine maintenance on your serger before you begin each project to minimize operating problems.

• **Brush out the area around the feed dogs.** This is even more important on a serger than on a sewing machine because the serger trims fabric, causing lint to accumulate quickly. This can jam the machine and reduce stitch quality.

• **Check the thread path or threading sequence.** Incorrect threading is a common problem, so it's a good idea to check each step.

• **Check the needles.** If your serger uses regular sewing machine needles, change the needles with each project. If the serger uses industrial needles, plan to change needles every two to three projects. If a needle is worn, damaged, or causes skipped stitches, replace it immediately, no matter how long it's been there!

The right presser foot can save you time and increase your creativity. Most of us use a standard all-purpose presser foot and a straight or zigzag stitch for 95% of our sewing projects. Yet the accessory box that comes with your sewing machine contains a vast array of presser feet. Start experimenting today—you'll discover new sewing shortcuts and expand your creative horizons!

A chart of sewing machine and serger feet begins on page 150.

• **Conventional, or general purpose, foot** is most commonly used for everyday sewing. Its wide opening is proportionate to the width of your machine's zigzag stitch (from 4 mm to 9 mm or $\frac{1}{8}$" to $\frac{1}{4}$", depending on the sewing machine). This foot is sometimes called a **zigzag foot**. Your machine's throat plate has an opening of similar size so that the needle can easily enter the bobbin area to form a perfect stitch.

• **Blindhem foot** is one of the most versatile feet in your accessory box. It is traditionally used for hemming woven and knit fabrics, but you can also use this presser foot to apply patch pockets and appliqués, and it makes straight edgestitching a breeze! Move the adjustable guide closer to or farther from the left side of the foot to accommodate fabrics of various weights and textures.

• **Buttonhole foot** makes it easy for you to sew identical buttonholes with smooth, uniform stitching, whether your project calls for two or twelve buttonholes. This foot moves forward and backward in a sliding tray attached to the machine. Markings along one or both sides of the foot indicate buttonhole length.

> ## Note from Nancy
>
> *The presser feet shown in the chart on page 150 may not look exactly like the feet in your accessory box because each manufacturer has a different style. To identify your presser feet, check your owner's manual, or compare the features listed in the chart with your presser feet.*

• **Cording foot** streamlines the process of making piping and of couching cords and trim to fabric. It's usually available from your sewing machine dealer. The top of the cording foot looks much like a conventional foot, with a wide opening for the zigzag stitch. However, the underside has a large, groove to accommodate cording, piping, or decorative trim, allowing the trim to lie flat and feed evenly under the foot.

• **Darning foot** has a spring that provides just the right amount of pressure on fabric to do free-motion embroidery. This transparent foot keeps the needle from drawing fabric up away from the feed dogs. The **Big Foot** is a large darning foot designed to provide more control.

• **Felling foot** is characterized by an opening or groove through which you can easily guide fabric to be turned under as it passes beneath the foot. As you might imagine, the felling foot was originally designed for making a flat-felled seam, a sturdy, decorative seam often used in sports clothing and children's wear. With this foot, you can easily duplicate these professionally tailored seams. For special accents, you can sew ribbon to fabric using the felling foot with a double needle.

> ## Note from Nancy
>
> *Depending on the position of the groove on your felling foot, you may need to change the position of the needles so that you center the ribbon between the double needles.*

• **Little Foot** makes it easy to get the accurate piecing that's crucial for successful quiltmaking. The right edge of the foot is precisely $\frac{1}{4}$" (6 mm) from the center needle position, providing an accurate mark for making a $\frac{1}{4}$" (6 mm) seam allowance. The left edge of the foot is precisely $\frac{1}{8}$" (3 mm) from the center needle position, providing an accurate mark for making a $\frac{1}{8}$" (3 mm) seam allowance. Red laser markings $\frac{1}{4}$" (6 mm) in front of and behind the needle serve as accurate reference points for starting, stopping, and pivoting when stitching $\frac{1}{4}$" seam allowances.

• **Multicord foot** guides up to five decorative threads under the foot to create unique embellishments. Some can accommodate up to nine

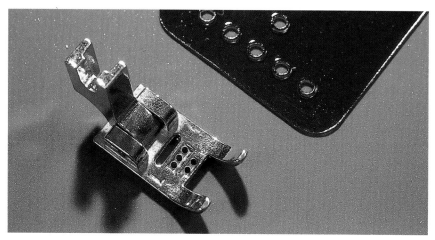

Multicord foot

threads. If you've ever wrestled with an assortment of decorative threads, trying to keep them aligned as you stitch them in place, you'll want to try this foot.

Use a **multiple cording guide** to keep threads aligned as they feed through the machine. This guide keeps threads separated and controls the flow so that your embellishment is even.

• **Open toe or embroidery foot** lets you see more of the area around the needle when sewing decorative stitches or when satin-stitching around appliqués. The toe area may be completely open, or its center may be clear plastic. This makes it easy to see stitches as they form on fabric. The underside has a hollowed or grooved section that lets dense stitching move smoothly under the foot without bunching beneath the needle.

• **Overcast-guide foot** has a special metal bar in the center of the foot's zigzag opening to hold fabric flat while the zigzag forms on the edge

of the fabric. Another vertical bar serves as a guide for fabric edges. If you don't own a serger and you find that zigzagged edges curl and pucker, try using an overcast-guide foot. It takes a little more time than serging, but you can simulate the appearance of a serged edge.

• **Pintuck foot** has a series of five to nine grooves on the underside that make sewing pintucks a snap. The grooves provide channels or guides for previous rows of pintucking, making it easy to guide and evenly space row after row of pintucks. By combining a pintuck foot with a double needle, you can quickly

make straight, uniform pintucks.

• **Sequins 'N Ribbon foot** has an adjustable guide to help you position trim precisely in front of the needle for effortless stitching. Sew on sequins, ribbons, and even narrow elastic with this unique presser foot.

• **Straightstitch or jean foot** is useful when stitching slippery fabrics, to prevent your fabric from being forced down into the feed dogs. This foot's tiny round opening minimizes puckering and creates a more uniformly balanced stitch. Use it with a throat plate that has a compatible round opening.

• **Tailor tack foot** has a vertical raised bar running down the center of the foot. The machine stitches over this bar, creating loops. This foot is a real time-saver when you're sewing on buttons and attaching shoulder pads.

• **Serger feet,** like sewing machine feet, are designed to simplify sewing specific types of projects. Commonly available serger feet include a beading foot, a blindhem foot, a cording or piping foot, an elastic foot, a ribbon foot, and a shirring or gathering foot.

pressing EQUIPMENT

For a truly professional-looking garment, press every step of the way. The difference between a truly professional-looking garment and one with a homemade look is often the way in which you press the garment. You cannot delay pressing until you complete the garment. Sew, then press! Press each seam or construction detail before you cross it with another seam or construction detail.

Basic tools and equipment make pressing easier and more efficient.

• A **steam iron** with a burst-of-steam feature provides optimum moisture. An adequate supply of steam eliminates the need for using a dampened press cloth with a dry iron. Your iron also needs a heavy soleplate for fusing interfacing.

Note from Nancy

On my public television series, "Sewing With Nancy," I use Rowenta irons. The amount of steam these irons produce far exceeds that of any other iron I have tried. The Dressmaker's Ham, Seam Roll, and press cloths I use are June Tailor products. All of these products—and the Deluxe Ironing Board I use— are available from the Nancy's Notions Sewing Catalog, as well as from sewing centers.

• Look for an **ironing board** that you can adjust up and down, for use standing or sitting, pressing or fusing interfacing. You must have a thickly padded ironing surface for proper fusing and bonding. Buy a pad specially made for that purpose, or cut up an old wool blanket to pad the ironing board.

Attach a bag or basket to hold scraps and waste thread. Fasten a pair of scissors to your ironing board with an elastic strip.

• A **seam roll** prevents seam imprints from showing on the right side of fabric. A purchased seam roll is sausage shaped and usually has wool fabric on one side and cotton drill on the other.

Although you can buy ready-made seam rolls through Nancy's Notions Sewing Catalog or at sewing centers, you can make your own. Tightly roll a magazine and cover it with fabric, or cover a yardstick with batting and fabric. This type of seam roll is perfect for pressing long seams in pants and skirts.

• A **press cloth** is essential for fusing interfacing and protecting the garment surface when pressing on the right side of fabric. Your press cloth should be lint-free and large enough to cover the area you're pressing. In addition to protecting the garment surface, a press cloth keeps the bottom of your iron clean when you're fusing.

A transparent cloth, such as the EZE-View Press Cloth, is helpful when fusing appliqués or doing other tasks where you need to see through your press cloth.

Woolen fabrics need a moisture-holding press cloth, such as the Steam 'n Shape Press Cloth.

Besides the essential pressing notions listed above, there are others you might find helpful.

• A **steam generator** consists of a lightweight iron plus a separate reservoir that holds more than a quart of water. The two are connected by a long, heavy-duty cable that houses both an electrical cord and a steam cord. The steam generator converts water from the reservoir into steam and passes it to the iron through the steam cord.

• A **sewing press** has a larger pressing surface than an iron and exerts up to 100 pounds of pressure.

• A **needleboard,** such as the Velvaboard, is a kind of press cloth with needlelike projections. Use it to press napped fabrics, such as velvet, as well as raised embellishments, such as silk ribbon.

• A **clapper** is a wooden block designed to help set seams and creases in heavy fabrics.

• A **tailor's ham** is similar to a seam roll, but it's designed for pressing and shaping set-in sleeves, darts, and curved seams.

• A **sleeve board** has a free-arm feature for pressing small openings and hard-to-reach areas.

FABRIC

For most sewers, a trip to the fabric store is a like a kid's trip to the candy store. You have all those wonderful wovens and knits to choose from—plaids and prints, solids and stripes, with butter-soft textures, nubby finishes, crisp body, or velvety nap. • **And then there are specialty fabrics**—luxurious Ultrasuede, cozy felt, fuzzy Polarfleece, and glamorous metallics. You can be a better sewer—and make your sewing easier— if you know at least the basics about these different fabrics. • **You'll even find variety in interfacings,** those lightweight supporting fabrics that add shape and body to garments. Choosing the right weight and type of interfacing is important to making a high-quality garment.

facts

Fabrics have fiber content and type. You might choose between linen suiting and wool suiting, rayon challis and silk challis, or 100%-cotton jersey and cotton-polyester jersey. Linen, wool, rayon, silk, cotton, and cotton/polyester are fibers, and suiting, challis, and jersey are fabric types.

Fiber content generally determines how you must launder a fabric. Each fabric bolt includes care instructions, often given in a numeric code. The following list gives the code numbers and explains what they mean.

1　Machine wash warm
2　Machine wash warm, line dry
3　Machine wash warm, tumble dry, remove promptly
4　Machine wash warm, delicate cycle, tumble dry low, use cool iron
5　Machine wash warm, do not dry-clean
6　Hand wash separately, use cool iron
7　Dry-clean only
8　Dry-clean pile fabric method only
9　Wipe with damp cloth only
10　Machine wash warm, tumble dry or line dry

Whenever you buy fabric, be sure to make a note of the appropriate care instructions. If you're making a garment or project for someone else, include a card with this information when you give the finished project.

The list of suggested fabrics included on your pattern can help you select the right one. You can

Checking Grain and Design

Before you buy any fabric, check to be sure the fabric ends are straight and that any printed design was applied straight. To check the ends:

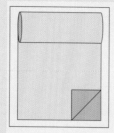 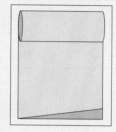

Diagram A: Line up fabric end with a table edge to be sure grain is straight.

• Line up the folded edge with the corner of a counter or table. Both ends of the folded fabric should be straight with the corner (*Diagram A*); if not, you may need to buy extra fabric.

• Look carefully at a printed design that is arranged in definite rows (*Diagram B*). If the rows are not straight both up and down and across the fabric, you may want to look for another fabric.

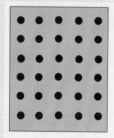 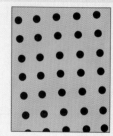

Diagram B: Be sure designs line up both up and down and across the fabric.

choose a fabric not listed on the pattern, but the list should help you understand the weight and drape of fabric the pattern designer recommends for that style. For example, if the pattern suggests lightweight to medium-weight fabrics such as chambray, cotton and cotton blends, and challis, you can assume that the dress may not drape well if you use a heavy wool or corduroy. Patterns also tell you which fabrics to avoid. (For example, "Not suitable for diagonals.")

Whenever you buy fabric, be sure to check the end of the bolt for appropriate laundry instructions.

woven FABRICS

Woven fabrics are made by interlacing threads. **The weight of the fabric varies depending on number of the threads used to weave it.** Wovens can be lightweight, such as batiste and organza, medium weight, such as broadcloth and challis, or heavyweight, such as denim and wool coating.

The lengthwise edges of woven fabric are called selvages. Selvages are more closely woven than the rest of the fabric (see *Photo* below). Since selvages tend to draw up with repeated laundering, don't include them in your project pieces.

All woven fabrics have grain, which is the direction in which the threads are woven. The threads of lengthwise grain run parallel to the selvages, and the threads of crosswise grain run from selvage to selvage. Bias is the diagonal line that runs at a 45° angle to the straight grain. For garments and other projects to drape properly, you must cut them either on the grain or on the bias, according to your pattern instructions.

Woven fabric cut on the bias has more stretch than the same fabric cut on the grain. To find true bias, begin at a corner of the fabric and measure the same distance along the selvage and across the crosswise grain. Connect those points. This line, which forms a 45° angle with the selvage, is true bias (*Diagram C*).

Woven fabrics are made from natural fibers, such as cotton, linen, wool, and ramie, or from synthetic fibers, such as acetate, rayon, nylon, and polyester. Many woven fabrics contain fiber blends, such as cotton/polyester and wool/acrylic. Silky fabrics, such as silk and satin, are woven, as are napped fabrics, such as velvet and corduroy. These fabrics require special sewing techniques. Information about them begins on page 26.

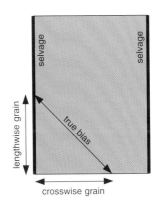

Diagram C: True bias is halfway between the selvage and the crosswise grain.

Note from Nancy

Synthetic fibers are usually made from chemical solutions containing products made from oil. These special liquids are forced through tiny holes and hardened to form continuous threads. Rayon (called viscose by British sewers) is a little different because it's made by adding chemicals to the natural cellulose found in wood.

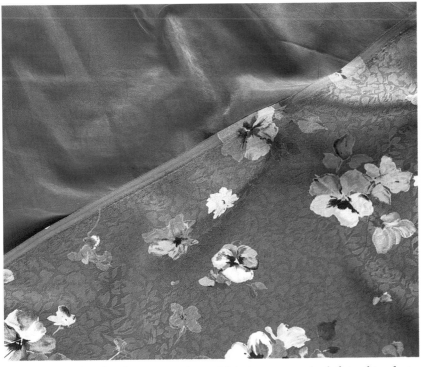

Selvages are the closely woven edges of fabric seen on the left in this photo.

You can't always tell by the look or feel of a fabric what its fiber content is, so be sure to read the label on the end of the fabric bolt. This label tells you laundering instructions as well as fabric content, fabric width, and other information.

Note from Nancy

When purchasing fabric, ask your clerk for a care label for the fabric you're buying. The store should be able to provide a label that you can sew into the garment.

When buying fabric for a project (woven or knit), remember that certain types require extra yardage. You will want to match plaids, stripes, diagonals, and large-scale prints, so you'll need enough fabric to adjust your layout for this. For napped fabrics, such as velveteen and corduroy, fabrics with finishes like satin and moiré, and one-way prints and jacquards, you need enough fabric to lay out all your pattern pieces in the same direction.

Pretreating and Storing Wovens

I recommend pretreating fabrics right after you buy them, so that they will be ready to stitch. You may question whether you need to do this, but the better-safe-than-sorry rule is "Pretreat the fabric as you expect to wash or clean the finished garment." Here's why:

All woven fabrics have grain, the direction in which the threads are woven.

• Shrink-resistant fabrics may shrink when machine-washed and dried. Even dry-clean-only fabrics should be professionally steamed, or at the very least, thoroughly steam-pressed at home. By removing any residual shrinkage before cutting out the garment, you ensure consistent fit throughout the life of the garment.
• Most fabric mills add finishes to fabrics to prevent soiling and wrinkling. Unfortunately, these resin finishes can also cause the machine to skip stitches. Pretreating fabrics helps remove those resins and prevents the aggravation of skipped stitches.
• By pretreating your fabric, you

can tell whether washing or steam pressing will remove the center crease and wrinkles. If the creases don't disappear, avoid those areas when laying out the pattern pieces.

To pretreat new fabric, launder washable fabrics in the delicate cycle of your washing machine. You don't have to wash a full cycle; a short cycle with a small amount of detergent works just as well and takes less time.

If the fabric ravels considerably, stitch the raw edges by zigzagging or serging them before washing.

Dry the fabric as you will dry the finished garment.

If you're not sure whether your fabric is washable, test a small piece before you launder the entire yardage. Cut a 4" square, and wash and dry it as you will launder the finished project. Then remeasure the square and compare it with the unwashed fabric. If it has shrunk considerably, changed shape, or faded significantly, plan to dry-clean the garment.

Before you store fabric, mark it to indicate that you've prewashed it. Cut off a small triangle at one corner of the yardage, and staple it to a file card along with the care instructions. You will be able to tell at a glance which fabric is prewashed and ready to stitch. Use the card to keep an organized record of your fabric stash.

See the fabric chart beginning on page 142 for information on needles and interfacings to use with different fabric types.

VERSATILE knits

My favorite clothes are my most comfortable ones, and for me, those are all knit: a fleece jumpsuit, a wool-jersey dress, a pair of interlock pants. Not only are knits comfortable, they are easy to fit. If, like many of us, your weight fluctuates, knit fabrics can expand to fit, hiding the changes.

Knit fabrics are made by pulling one loop of yarn or thread through another loop, creating a stretchy construction. Like woven fabrics, they can be made from natural fibers (cotton, silk, wool), synthetic fibers (rayon, polyester, acrylic), or a blend of fibers. As a rule, knits resist wrinkles more than wovens, but they do not crease as well. Knits don't ravel, but some run and many curl at cut edges.

Interlock and jersey are the most common forms of knits, but you may also find sweater knits, sweatshirt knits, tricot, and other types of knit fabrics. Sweater knits look and stretch like hand-knit fabrics. Sweatshirt knits are single knits that have a napped surface on the right or wrong side of the fabric. Tricot is a lightweight knit that is resistant to runs and is often used for lingerie and loungewear.

Ribbings are knits that have alternating ribs and wales that form pronounced vertical ridges. They look the same on both sides. Ribbings are used to finish garments at the neck, waist, or hem. Once reserved for use with knit fabrics, ribbings are showing up more and more on the edges of woven garments. Ribbings vary in stretch from 25% to 100%, and some tend to run badly. You should always sew them using a zigzag stitch, a stretch stitch, or a serger.

See the chart on page 142 for information about needles and interfacings to use with different types of knits.

Interlock Knits

Manufacturers create interlock knits by interlocking two yarn loops, one from the back and one from the front of the fabric (*Diagram A* on page 24). Classified as double knits, interlock knits look the same on the right and wrong sides of the fabric. They have little crosswise stretch but stretch lengthwise and on the bias.

Knits are comfortable and easy to sew.

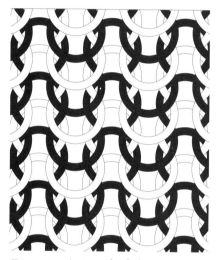

Diagram A: Interlock knit construction

Knits are ideal for making casual wear, such as T-shirts.

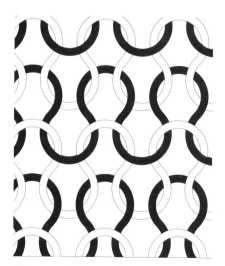

Diagram B: Jersey knit construction

Many people prefer 100%-cotton interlock knit, which is less clingy and less prone to pilling than a cotton-polyester blend. However, all-cotton interlock is more expensive than a blend and may shrink more. An interlock blend made from 50% cotton and 50% polyester is more affordable, shrinks less, and comes in a wider assortment of colors than the all-cotton variety.

Jersey Knits

Jersey is a single-knit fabric formed from one set of yarn loops (*Diagram B*). This construction makes jersey smooth on the right side, with horizontal loops running crosswise on the wrong side. The yarn loops can be very fine, so it may be hard to distinguish between the two sides.

To determine the right side of a jersey knit, hold a cut edge (either crossgrain or selvage) and pull to stretch the edge. Jersey always rolls to the right side.

Fiber content varies for jersey knits. They can be made from acrylic, wool, cotton, or blends. Wool and wool-like (acrylic) jerseys have the greatest body and the least tendency to roll or curl. Cotton and cotton-polyester jerseys are lighter in weight, making them well suited for use in T-shirts and children's wear but often too limp for use in dresses or skirts. Blends of cotton and Lycra (usually 10% to 15% Lycra) are ideal for stretch pants and activewear.

Polarfleece

One of the more popular types of knit that isn't an interlock or a jersey is Polarfleece. This lightweight, high-loft 100%-polyester knit offers warmth without weight. It is popular for outerwear because it doesn't readily absorb moisture. Brand names for Polarfleece include Tundra Fleece, Arctic Fleece, and Polartec. Like many knits, Polarfleece is usually 60" (152.5 cm) wide. It has a lot of crosswise stretch, while the lengthwise grain is relatively stable.

Pretreating and Storing Knits

Pretreat washable interlocks by laundering the fabric as you will the finished garment. For best results, pretreat any 100%-cotton interlock by washing and drying it twice. This double washing eliminates residual shrinkage and compacts the yarns in the knit, adding body to the finished garment.

To pretreat washable jersey, machine-launder the fabric as you will the finished garment. If the fabric is 80% or more cotton, it may shrink up to 10%.

When you use wool jersey, always have it steamed by a dry cleaner. Steaming preshrinks the fabric and removes surface sizing.

Store knit fabrics as you do wovens. (See page 22.)

Determining Stretch Percentage

Not all knits stretch the same amount. The fiber content and type of knit construction dictates the amount of stretch.

Check your pattern to see if it states the amount of stretch required (for example, "25% stretch" or "50% stretch"). Look for a stretch gauge on the back of your pattern envelope; if it has one, be sure you have it with you when you buy the fabric for the pattern.

To determine the amount of stretch of a knit fabric:

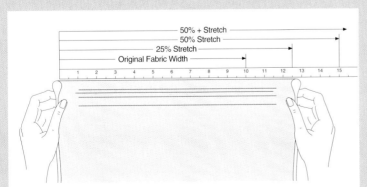

1. Fold under 3" along the cut edge of the fabric (the crosswise grain) to prevent the cut edge from stretching excessively during the test.

2. Pull 10" of the fabric to see how far it stretches (*Diagram C*).
   10" stretches to 12½" = 25% stretch
   10" stretches to 15" = 50% stretch

Diagram C: Measure 10" of fabric to see how far it stretches.

specialty FABRICS

Today's specialty fabrics—such as felts, laces and netting, metallics, real and synthetic animal skins, and fleece—are easy to sew, but may require special equipment or techniques. Some woven and knit fabrics also require special handling when sewing. These include napped fabrics, such as velvet and velveteen, and slippery fabrics, such as satin and tricot knits.

Felts

Felt is a nonwoven fabric usually made from wool, acrylic, or a fiber blend. It has no bias, no grain, and no right or wrong side. Felt is made by using moisture, heat, and pressure to fuse loose fibers together, which are then pounded to force them closer together.

Acrylic felts are washable and usually much less expensive than 100%-wool felts. Craft and fabric stores often carry acrylic felts in a wide variety of colors, by the yard or in various-size pieces.

Wool felt is also washable but it shrinks. To make a finished garment machine washable, prewash wool felt in cold water on a gentle cycle, and dry it on a permanent press or delicate setting.

Note from Nancy

Prewashing wool felt causes as much as 75% shrinkage. If you plan to avoid dry-cleaning your finished project by prewashing, buy extra felt.

Felt is easy to sew. It doesn't ravel or fray, so you don't have to finish the edges. However, it does tend to bag at stress points, such as knees, elbows, and seat, and is difficult to mend.

Felted fabrics are knitted or woven fabrics made from wool or other fibers that have been shrunk and pounded to make them feltlike. These fabrics (such as Polarfleece and boiled wool) have the fray-proof edges and ease of sewing of true felt, but they usually wear much better than felt. Felted fabrics also cost more than true felt.

Laces and Nets

Lace can be anything from a very fine, sheer trim to a heavy decorative fabric. Net is open-mesh fabric often used for bridal and formal wear.

Lace can be made from cotton, silk, linen, metallic threads, or a variety of other natural and synthetic threads. It may be woven, embroidered, or knotted. Lace is sheer or transparent, and since the edges usually don't ravel, you can leave them unfinished. When stitching seams, make them very narrow. Lace doesn't have a grain, but it often has one-way designs, so you may need to buy extra yardage.

Some laces are made on a background of net. Plain net is used for bridal veils (illusion); undergarments or yokes on formal gowns (English net); and petticoats, skirt ruffles, trims, and interfacing for sheer or fine fabrics (bobbinet and tulle). Like lace, net doesn't have a true grain and does not ravel. Net

does stretch more on the crosswise grain than on the lengthwise grain. Cut all pattern pieces either on the lengthwise grain or tilted as needed from the lengthwise grain. Don't mix lengthwise and crosswise grain when cutting pieces.

Since net is transparent, if you finish seams, make 1/8" (3 mm) French seams, or bind the edges with tricot or another soft fabric. Net tears easily, so stitch with care.

Metallics

Metallic fabrics are usually made from a blend of aluminum or plastic threads with polyester, nylon, rayon, silk, wool, or cotton. They can be woven or knitted to create fabrics that vary in weight from tissue lamé to heavy brocades.

Metallic fabrics fray and snag easily and can be scratchy. Use needles especially made for metallic fabrics, because regular sewing needles dull quickly and tend to snag or pull the fabric. Check the fabric bolt label carefully, because some metallic fabrics are hard to clean. Newer metallic fabrics won't tarnish like older ones did, because they're made from non-tarnishing metal or plastic.

Synthetic and Real Animal Skins

The first clothes were made from animal skins, and we still use leather, suede, chamois, and other tanned hides for garments. But today, synthetic animal skins are more popular than the real thing.

Real or synthetic animal skins, such as Ultrasuede, don't ravel, so you can leave edges unfinished.

Synthetic suede, such as Ultrasuede, is one of my favorite specialty fabrics. It's lovely, luxurious, and easy to sew, and it's even washable. Synthetic suedes cost $40 to $50 a yard. To save money, use small amounts for small projects or to make unusual embellishments. Save yardage on other projects by using seam allowances smaller than ⅝" (1.5 cm). The fabric won't ravel, so a ⅜" to ½" (9 mm to 1.3 cm) seam should work.

Synthetic suede is available in several weights from suit weight to featherweight. Ultrasuede is 100% polyester and comes in many brilliant colors, prints, and textures. It's made through a nonwoven process.

Real and synthetic animal skins do not fray, so you don't need to finish the edges. You may also eliminate facings and such garment construction elements as under collars.

Pins and machine stitching make permanent holes in these fabrics. Keep sewing details and use of pins to a minimum by using alternative methods whenever practical. For example, use a fabric glue stick to temporarily bond layers rather than pinning them. Because needle holes are permanent, you cannot let out an animal skin garment.

For sewing **real leather**, use a leather needle in your machine. This wedge-shaped needle makes a large hole that will eventually tear in synthetic suede or leather. See the needle chart on page 149 for information on needles.

A hot iron damages animal skins (real or synthetic), so keep pressing to a minimum. Never place the iron directly on the fabric's right side, and always use a heavy press cloth. Use lots of steam to press Ultrasuede, but do not use steam to press leather, real or synthetic. Rather than bonding Ultrasuede appliqués using fusible web, which you press before and after removing the paper backing, use liquid iron-on adhesive, such as LiquiFuse.

Napped and Pile Fabrics

Melton, camel's hair, mohair, brushed denim, and sweatshirt fleece are napped fabrics. Chenille, corduroy, fake fur, fleece, terry, and velvet are pile fabrics.

The fiber ends of napped fabrics are raised to the surface, then clipped, brushed flat, or left erect. Pile fabrics are knitted or woven with an extra set of yarns to make pile on one or both sides of the fabric. The pile can be cut or uncut, over the entire surface or in selected areas to form patterns.

These fabrics reflect light differently from different positions, so you must cut pattern pieces in the same direction. You usually need more fabric to accommodate this special layout. Patterns that suggest napped or pile fabrics usually provide napped layout diagrams and extra yardage requirements.

Pins and changes in seam lines easily mar these fabrics. Also, take special care when pressing napped or pile fabrics. Use a needleboard (see page 17) and a press cloth, and press from the wrong side. Test the heat, amount of steam, and pressure on scraps before pressing your project.

Some napped and pile fabrics can be slippery to sew. See below for tips on handling slippery fabrics.

Slippery Fabrics

Some woven or knitted fabrics have slippery surfaces, due either to the nature of their fibers or their construction. These include sateen, satin, silk, taffeta, and tricot knits.

Slippery fabrics snag easily and ravel badly. They're susceptible to marring by pins, needles, and even rough hands. Removed seams are easily visible. Pin these types of fabrics using silk pins or fine needles.

Slippery fabrics don't ease well, so choose a pattern with little easing at sleeves and seams. If your machine doesn't have dual feed (to feed fabric from both top and bottom), use a walking foot or a jeans foot to hold the fabric firmly. To prevent seams from puckering, hold fabric taut as it feeds through the machine.

Interfacings are hidden inside garments, but they're essential to good construction. Patterns list the amount of interfacing you need in a yardage chart on the back of the envelope. Choose an interfacing that is lighter in weight than your fabric.

You can buy woven or nonwoven interfacings, fusible or nonfusible, in weights from sheer to heavy. Choose white, gray, beige, or black to most closely match your fabric.

Weights and Types

The key to using interfacing successfully is to choose the correct weight and type for your fabric. Care instructions for interfacing should be the same as those for your garment fabric. The weight of the interfacing should complement and reinforce the weight and shape of your garment fabric.

See the fabric chart on page 142 for help in choosing the right fusible interfacing to match your fabric.

Fusible interfacings are great for stabilizing knit garments in areas that easily sag or stretch out of shape. For example, stabilize knit pants to prevent sagging in the knee area by fusing interfacing to the wrong side of the fabric from 4" above to 4" below the stress point of the knee. You can prevent pockets from stretching by fusing a ¾"-wide bias strip of interfacing to the wrong side of the pocket, even with the cut edge. Stabilize shoulder seams by fusing a ¾"-wide strip of interfacing (cut on the length-wise grain) to the shoulder seams on the front only.

Quick-and-easy fusible interfacings give more rigidity to fabric than nonfusibles. The difference between fusible interfacing and fusible web is that fusible interfacing has adhesive on one side only, and fusible web has adhesive on both sides.

Manufacturers apply fusible resins to interfacing fabrics by one of two processes.

• **Dot application:** During this process, which is similar to printing, adhesive resins are applied to the interfacing through a fine mesh screen on a roller. The dots are uniform throughout the interfacing, providing consistent high quality. To identify this type of interfacing, look for the series of dots on the wrong side of the interfacing (Diagram).

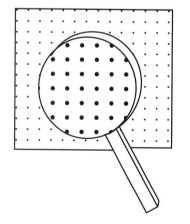

Diagram: Fusible adhesive may be applied to interfacing in dots.

• **Allover application:** Powdered resin is sprinkled on the wrong side of the interfacing base fabric. A roller passes over the fabric, attaching the adhesives to the fabric. Allover application interfacings are inexpensive, but the amount of resin and its placement on the fabric may vary from area to area.

Base Fabrics

All fusible interfacings begin with a base fabric. This fabric may be nonwoven, woven, knit, or weft-insertion. Each has particular characteristics and is suited for specific purposes.

The majority of interfacings have nonwoven bases. Nylon, polyester, or a blend of fibers is processed much like felt (with heat, moisture, and pressure) to make a nonravel-ling fabric. Some are stable in both length and width; others stretch in one or more directions.

Most ready-to-wear garments have **stretch nonwoven interfacings**. These have crosswise stretch and lengthwise stability and are suited to areas that require specific support and shaping.

All-bias nonwoven interfacings provide supple shaping or general overall shaping. You can cut them in any direction.

Stable nonwoven interfacings stretch in neither length nor width and are intended specifically for tailoring.

Woven interfacings are stable both crosswise and lengthwise, but they do stretch on the bias.

For greater drapability and softer shaping, cut woven interfacings on the bias.

Knit interfacings have a 100%-nylon tricot base. They are the most flexible of all interfacings and provide the softest shaping. Knit interfacings are stable lengthwise but stretch on the crosswise grain. Use them to stabilize loosely woven knit fabrics, to underline fabrics, and to reinforce areas, especially on knit fabrics.

Take a tricot fabric base, insert a series of yarns in the crosswise (weft) direction, and you get **weft-insertion interfacing**. This type of interfacing is stable both lengthwise and crosswise, providing a firm yet supple shaping. It drapes

Interfacings add body and shape to any type of fabric.

like a knit, but offers the stability of a woven. Weft-insertion interfacings are well suited for tailoring.

Buying and Pretreating Interfacings

Save yourself time and effort by purchasing three to five yards of your favorite interfacing at once. You'll have interfacing available when you need it.

To store interfacing, roll it onto a tube (to prevent wrinkles and save space). Tuck inside the roll the interfacing interleaf with instructions for fusing.

Even if you always pretreat fabric, you may not have thought about pretreating interfacing. Not all interfacings require pretreating. At Nancy's Notions, we tested interfacing samples to develop the following recommendations:

1. **Do not pretreat nonwoven fusible interfacings.** They do not shrink, probably because the high heat used to apply the fusible resins to the fabric base has already shrunk the interfacing. The ready-to-wear industry routinely uses non-wovens without pretreating them.

2. **Pretreat knit, woven, and weft-insertion fusible interfacings** using the process below. Our test samples shrunk about 2% with this process, primarily in length.
• Immerse the interfacing in a basin of warm water, and allow the water to cool.
• Remove from water and roll in a terry towel to remove excess water.

• Hang or air dry the interfacing.

Fusing Restrictions
You can use fusible interfacings for about 90% of your sewing projects. However, fusibles are not suited for the following fabrics:
• **Heavily textured fabrics,** such as tapestry and seersucker, because fusing flattens the surface of the fabric.
• **Fabrics that are sensitive to heat, moisture, and pressure,** such as velvet and some silks, because fusing alters the surface.
• **Fabrics treated with stain- or water-repellent finishes,** because the silicone treatment repels the moisture needed to bond fusibles.

Test-Fusing Interfacing
Fusibles can change the character of the fabrics to which they are fused. To be sure a particular interfacing is suited to your fabric, test it first. It's time well spent.

> ### Note from Nancy
>
> *Make sure your test fabric pieces are large enough so that you can tell whether the interfacing reacts as you want it to in a completed garment. I use enough fashion fabric so that I can fold an unfused garment section over the fused section to duplicate how the finished garment will feel.*

Test fusibles as follows:

1. Cut test strips of the fabric and of one or more interfacings.

• Cut 4" to 6" (10 cm to 15 cm) squares of interfacing.

• Cut 5" to 10" (12.5 cm to 25 cm) strips of fabric, or use fabric scraps.

• Cut 1" fabric squares for tabs. You will pull on these tabs to check the bond after fusing.

2. Test-fuse the interfacing to the fabric.

• Press the wrong side of the fashion fabric to warm it and make it more receptive to fusing.

• Place interfacing samples on the fabric with a tab underneath one interfacing corner (*Diagram A*).

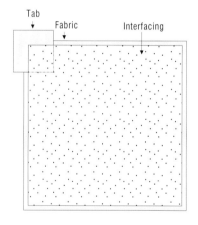

Diagram A: Place a fabric tab at the corner for test fusing.

• Cover with a damp press cloth.

Note from Nancy

Using a damp press cloth is very important! Heat and moisture activate the resins used on interfacings. Unless you use adequate moisture for fusing, the bond will not be secure.

• Fuse for 10 to 15 seconds with the iron temperature set at wool. (Check the interfacing bolt for specific instructions; if they differ from these, follow the manufacturer's instructions.) Use an up-and-down motion rather than sliding your iron.

• Turn the sample upside down and fuse again. This draws the resin through the fibers, creating a better bond.

• Allow the sample to dry and cool.

3. Examine the sample.

• Check the bond. Pull the fabric tab to see if the interfacing is firmly bonded. If it peels away, fuse again, using more heat, pressure, and time.

• Check the fabric for puckers or wrinkles. If you find them, try increasing pressure. If this doesn't correct the problem, your interfacing may be too heavy.

• Check for interfacing bubbles. Bubbles may mean that your iron is too hot. Using a press cloth helps reduce this problem.

• Check the right side of the fabric for color changes.

• Check the hand (feel) of the interfaced fabric, and compare it with that of uninterfaced fabric. Is it too stiff? Is it stiff enough?

Note from Nancy

Less is usually best when it comes to interfacing. As a general rule, choose interfacing that's lighter in weight than your fashion fabric. Just remember your purpose. Do you want soft shaping? Are you trying to support or stabilize a specific area? Do you want to add crispness to pattern details?

Double Fusing

Most of the time, you'll use only one layer of interfacing. However, sometimes it's helpful to use two layers, such as for reinforcing buttonholes. Here's how:

1. Cut interfacing patches 1½" wide and 1" longer than the buttonhole. Use the same interfacing that you use for the facing. Pink the edges so that they will be more diffused and less visible.

2. After applying interfacing to the facing, fuse patches of interfacing where you will place the buttonholes (*Diagram B*). This double layer provides extra support.

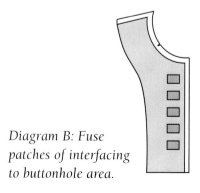

Diagram B: Fuse patches of interfacing to buttonhole area.

Quick Fusing Technique

Getting a quick, durable bond is easy if you follow a few basic steps.

1. Lower your ironing board, if possible (*Diagram A*). This makes it easier for you to lean into the iron, providing greater leverage, which gives you a more permanent bond.

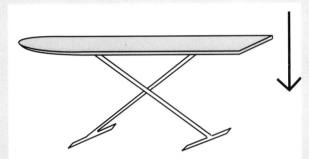

Diagram A: Lower your ironing board.

2. Iron the wrong side of the fabric to warm it and make it more receptive to fusing.

3. Position the interfacing on the wrong side of the facing, fusible side down (*Diagram B*).

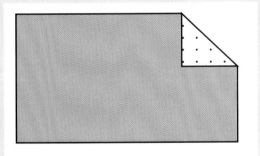

Diagram B: Position interfacing.

4. Cover the interfacing with a damp press cloth. This prevents scorching and adds moisture, which is essential for a proper bond.

5. When fusing large pieces of interfacing, use the tip of the iron to steam-baste the interfacing to the fashion fabric in several areas (*Diagram C*). This keeps the interfacing from shifting when you start to fuse.

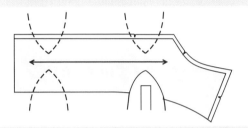

Diagram C: Steam-baste large pieces of interfacing.

6. Fuse interfacing to the garment, following the manufacturer's directions. Usually, this means pressing for 10 to 15 seconds with the iron on wool setting. Lean into the iron for more pressure.

7. With large interfacing pieces, fuse one section, and then fuse the adjoining section, overlapping the first fused area. Overlapping ensures a proper bond. Repeat until the entire piece is fused.

8. Turn the fabric over. Repeat the process on the right side to draw resins deeper into the fabric and to create a stronger bond.

Note from Nancy

Small pieces of interfacing may stick out beyond your fabric facings. To keep these from fusing to your ironing board, cover the board with an appliqué pressing sheet. After you fuse the interfacing and it cools, you can easily peel it from the sheet and trim the excess.

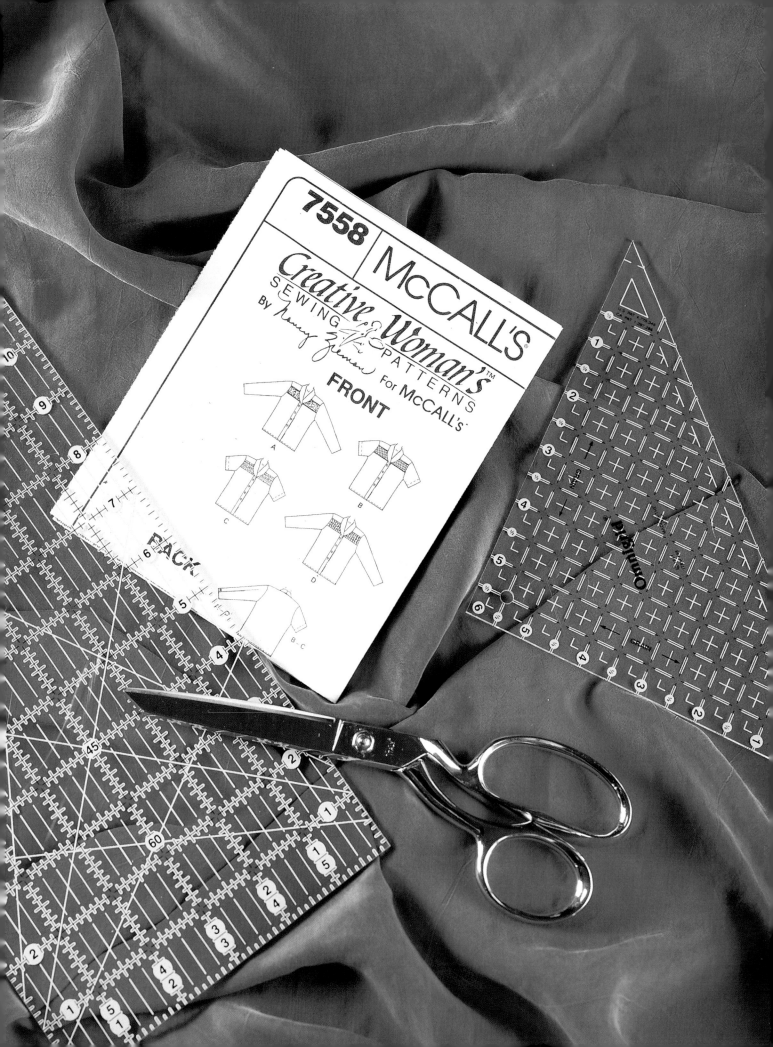

PATTERNS

Patterns are the "road maps" that show us how to get from flat fabric to a finished garment or other project. Starting with photos or drawings of the finished project on the envelope, each pattern has a wealth of purchasing and sewing information. • **I've been known to fall in love with a fabric** and then search for just the right pattern to use, but I usually find the pattern first and look for fabric to match. The pattern envelope has so much useful information, from suggested fabric types to a list of required notions! • **For your garment to fit**, you have to choose the right size and pattern type. Then you must lay out and cut your pattern pieces with care.

pattern

Which pattern you choose depends on such factors as style preference, fabric choice, even how much time you have to make the project. My guidelines can help you select one that requires the fewest alterations.

Accurate Measurements

To know what size to buy, take several measurements (Diagram A). If you're buying a different size pattern than you have in the past or if you're new to sewing, take all measurements. If your pattern size hasn't changed, measure only areas you know are too tight, too loose, too long, or too short.

Diagram A: Start by measuring bust (1), waist (2), hip (3), back waist length (4), and height (5).

• **Bust:** Measure around the fullest part, keeping the tape measure parallel to the floor (Diagram B). Measure to the closest 1/2" (1.3 cm). When taking width measurements,

place a thumb or finger under the tape measure to avoid measuring too tightly (Diagram C).

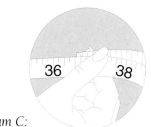

Diagram B: Measure fullest part of bust.

Diagram C:
Keep finger under
tape to prevent measuring too tightly.

Note from Nancy

Don't worry about fractions less than 1/2". Measurements fluctuate. Remember what an extra piece of chocolate cake can do to the fit of your waistband.

• **Waist:** To take this measurement, bend to the side; the deepest wrinkle is your waist (Diagram D). Stand straight again and measure around your waist, keeping the tape measure parallel to the floor. Place your thumb or a finger under the tape measure to avoid taking the measurement too tightly. Measure to the closest 1/2" (1.3 cm).

Diagram D: Bend to the side to find your true waist.

• **Hip:** Measure the fullest part of the hip, keeping the tape measure parallel to the floor and your finger under the tape to make sure it's not too tight. Measure to the closest 1/2" (1.3 cm).
• **Hip Length:** Measure the distance between your waist and your hip. This measurement lets you mark hipline placement, allowing you to add to or subtract from the pattern at your actual hip.

Note from Nancy

When I measure the width around my hip, I simply pick up the loose end of the tape measure to measure the distance between my waist and hip (Diagram E).

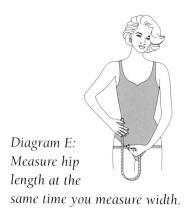

Diagram E:
Measure hip length at the
same time you measure width.

• **Back Waist Length**: Measure from the base of your neck to your waist. Find the base of your neck by bending your head forward until you can easily feel the prominent bone at the base of your neck. Straighten your neck and measure from that bone down your back to your waist.

• **Back Width**: Measure from one side to the other across the back, directly above the arm creases.

• **Sleeve Length**: Have your friend feel for the knob at the end of your shoulder and keep a finger there. (Depending on your body, it may help to raise your elbow as high as your shoulder.) Then place a hand on your hip. Have your friend measure from your shoulder knob over the elbow to your wrist bone. (Measuring with your arm bent builds in ease for your sleeve.)

• **Upper Arm Width**: Measure the fullest part of your arm between the shoulder and the elbow, with a finger under the tape measure to make sure it's not too tight. Measure to the closest ½" (1.3 cm).

• **Height**: Stand barefoot with your back to a wall. Lay a ruler flat on top of your head. Mark where it touches the wall. Then measure from the mark to the floor.

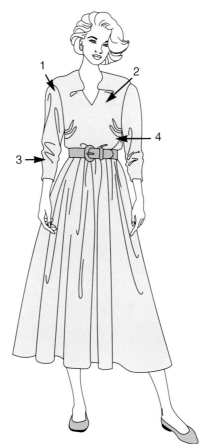

Diagram F: Gaposis results when high bust doesn't fit properly. Signs include garment shoulder not matching figure (1), neckline gapping from too much fabric (2), sleeve wrinkles caused by poor fit (3), and garment folds at underarms (4).

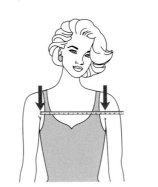

Diagram G: Take the front-width measurement to determine size.

Preventing Gaposis

If your body proportions are average, compare your measurements with those on the back of the pattern to choose the correct size. See page 36 for information about pattern types.

But if your bust is large in proportion to the rest of your body, or if you have a broad back, you may have found that using the standard system to choose a pattern size (using your bust measurement) doesn't work for you. The pattern fits your bust, but gaps at the neckline, the shoulders, and the armholes (*Diagram F*).

"Gaposis," as I call it, is a common fitting problem that's hard to correct. The solution? Buy your pattern to fit your shoulder area.

I recommend using the front-width measurement to determine which pattern size fits your shoulders. You won't find this measurement on the back of the pattern envelope, but it's quick to take and doesn't change, even if you gain or lose weight.

Here's how to take the front-width measurement:

• Find the crease in the skin where your arm meets your body.

• Measure above the end of one crease straight across the front of your chest to the end of the other crease (*Diagram G*). Round off the measurement to the nearest ½".

Front-Width Fitting Chart

Front Width	12"	12½"	13"	13½"	14"	14½"	15"	15½"	16"	16½"	17"	17½"	18"
Misses'/Petite	6	8	10	12	14	16	18	20	22				
Juniors	5	7	9	11	13	15							
Half Size			10½	12½	14½	16½	18½	20½	22½	24½			
Women's							38	40	42	44	46	48	50

Choose your correct blouse, dress, or jacket size by taking your front-width measurement (see page 35) and using this chart.

Even though the front-width measurement and its corresponding size don't appear on the back of a pattern envelope, it's easy to determine what size to buy. A 14" front-width measurement equals size 14. Add one size for each ½" over 14"; subtract one size for each ½" under 14". For example, if your front-width measurement is 13½", buy size 12. See the chart above.

Note from Nancy

If you're unsure which of two sizes to use, go with the smaller size. Remember, it's easier to fit the bust (make it larger) than to fit the neckline and shoulders.

You may be pleasantly surprised by the results you get using the front-width measurement. It's very common for someone who has been sewing with a size 20 in order to fit her bust to find out she is actually a size 16.

Pattern Types

Your body proportions determine the type of pattern that will fit you best. The back of each company's pattern catalog provides the standard body measurement charts that company uses. Compare the height, the back waist length measurement, and the description of the pattern type to your own measurements.

Patterns for women come in five size categories, each designed for women with different proportions: Misses', Petite or Petite-able, Half Size, Women's, and Juniors.

Note from Nancy

You can also find size charts for toddlers, children, teens, boys, and men in the back of most pattern catalogs. There are also pattern companies for large women's sizes, such as Great Fit, that specialize in sizes 38 to 60.

• **Misses'** patterns are for women with well-proportioned and well-developed figures, approximately 5'5" to 5'6", who wear a B cup bra size. Back waist length is 9".

Note from Nancy

If your bust measurement is more than 2½" larger than your high bust measurement (Diagram A), you are larger than a B cup size.

Diagram A: Measure your high bust line (2) and compare it to your bust line measurement (1) to determine cup size.

• **Petite** sizes are for women who are approximately 5'2" to 5'3" and are similarly proportioned to the Misses' figure. Bust, waist, and hip measurements are the same as for Misses' patterns. Back waist length is 7".

• **Juniors** patterns are for well-proportioned, shorter-waisted figures, approximately 5'4" to 5'5", with an A–B cup bra size. A Juniors size 7 corresponds to a Misses' size 8. Back waist length is 7".

• **Half Size** patterns have more room in the bust, waist, and hip, and shorter length proportions. They are designed for women between 5'2" and 5'4", with a C cup bra size. Back waist length is 7".

• **Women's** patterns are for figures the same height as the Misses' (5'5" to 5'6"), but they are fuller and larger in the bust (D cup), waist, and hip. Back waist length is 9".

When buying patterns for skirts and pants, choose size based on which measurement is critical to the garment's fit. For example, choose the size that fits your hip if the style is tailored through the hipline. Or choose by the waistline measurement if the waist is fitted and the hipline is gathered. If you're taller than 5'6" or shorter than 5'2", buy the pattern style that fits your proportions and alter the length.

Altering a Pattern

Few of us are a perfect size 10. To make a pattern fit, most of us need to add to one body area or subtract from another. It takes about 20 minutes to make minor alterations to your pattern, readying it for layout and cutting.

Use your favorite method of altering the pattern to your measurements and height. If you generally use patterns from the same company (such as Butterick or McCall's), you may be able to repeat the same basic alterations from garment to garment.

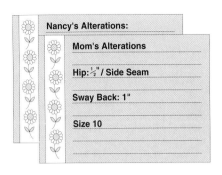

Diagram B: Use a recipe card file to record fitting information.

> ### Note from Nancy
>
> *Use waxed paper and permanent felt-tip pens for altering patterns. They are inexpensive and readily available. Another plus: After you finish marking the alterations, you can easily fuse the waxed paper to the original pattern, using a warm, dry iron. My book,* Fitting Finesse, *explains in detail my favorite alterations method, the pivot-and-slide technique.*

A recipe card file is an efficient way to keep track of the alterations you make (*Diagram B*). Date the card so that you can see at a glance when you last used the pattern. If you have gained or lost weight since that time, the card will alert you to readjust your alterations before using the pattern again.

Save time by adding recipe cards for others, too. If you sew for your children, mother, husband, other relatives, or friends, these cards will serve as quick references for necessary alterations.

You may be able to reduce the number of alterations you need by choosing a pattern style that isn't closely fitted where your measurements differ from the pattern's. For example, if your waist measurement is the same as the pattern but your hips are a little larger or smaller, choose a skirt or dress pattern that has a fitted waist and a pleated or gathered skirt. Try a blouse with shoulder tucks instead of darts if your bust measurement is a little different from the pattern's.

If your measurements differ by more than 1" from the pattern, you'll probably need to alter to fit rather than counting on the style to camouflage your figure differences.

Diagram: Design ease is extra room that lets you move in clothes.

Design Ease

All patterns are designed with ease—a little extra room that provides both comfort and fashion. The amount of ease varies depending upon the style and the type of fabric for which the pattern was designed (*Diagram*).

Design ease is the difference between the measurements on the back of the pattern, which apply to all patterns from that company, and the actual measurements of the tissue pattern, which apply only to the style you purchased.

Most of the time, you won't need to check the pattern tissue measurements for the amount of design ease. However, if you think an oversize style may have too much ease, or a form-fitting style may not have enough ease, it's a good idea to check the measurements.

For woven fabrics, the minimum ease requirements are:

Bust: 3" to 4"

Waist: 1/2" to 1"

Hip: 3" to 4"

Designers use these amounts as guidelines, varying the actual ease to give fashion and style to patterns. A loose-fitting jacket, for example, might have as much as 6" to 8" of bust ease. That means that if a closer-fitting dress seemed only a little snug when you made it according to the company's pattern, you may not need to alter the looser-fitting jacket.

Most pattern manufacturers now print the finished garment measurements on the back of the pattern envelope or on the guide sheet inside the pattern. Compare these measurements to the body measurements for the same size (also listed on the back of the pattern envelope). The difference between the two is the amount of ease built into the pattern. If your body measurements are between pattern sizes, the amount of ease the pattern provides might help you decide which pattern size to use.

Shopping Tips

Pattern catalogs and magazines offer an enticing selection of ready-to-sew fashions. Because your pattern will be the road map for your project, the catalog area should be your first stop at the fabric store.

The pattern envelope offers a wealth of valuable information, so study both the front and the back of the envelope carefully. The front shows photos or sketches (called "views") of all the style variations included in the pattern. These views usually show the garment from the front.

The back of the pattern envelope includes detailed purchasing and sewing information (*Photo*, page 39).

• **Back view:** Back views may be illustrated on the back of the envelope. Details such as darts, pockets, and variations in length are easily distinguished at a glance.

• **Body measurements:** The envelope has a concise chart of body measurements, usually including bust, waistline, and hipline measurements, along with corresponding pattern sizes.

• **Suggested fabrics:** This section contains essential information— the designer's fabric recommendations. It also tells you which fabrics are less likely to work for this pattern style. Phrases like "for stretch knits only" and "not suitable for diagonals" provide important information for you to use in fabric selection.

• **Yardage chart:** To determine the amount of fabric and interfacing to buy, you must know three things: the pattern view (generally designated by a letter), your size, and the fabric width. Under the desired view, follow the size chart down and the fabric width chart across. The columns intersect at the yardage requirement.

• **Notions:** The notions you need to complete the garment—buttons, snaps, hooks and eyes, zippers, elastic, and thread—are listed in this section.

• **Finished garment measurements:** These measurements are important! Compare them to the body measurements for the same size; the difference between the two measurements is the amount of ease or "living room" the pattern allows. See page 38 for more information about design ease.

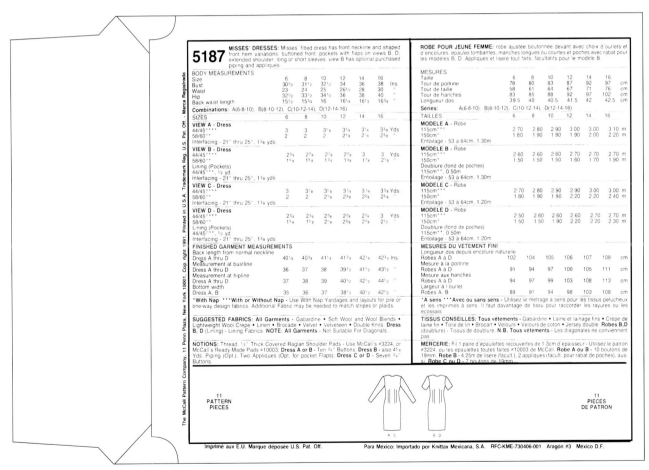

The back of the pattern envelope provides information on body measurements, fabrics, yardage required, notions, and more, along with drawings of the back view of the garment.

Before you can lay out your pattern for cutting, you must prepare your fabric. If you didn't pretreat the fabric when you bought it, see page 22 for instructions on prewashing wovens and page 25 for prewashing knits.

Spread your fabric out to see if it has a prominent crease where it was folded. Press it according to the care instructions. If this center crease does not press out, you will have to adjust your cutting layout to avoid using the crease in your finished garment.

Carefully refold the fabric, matching selvages and keeping the grain line straight. If the fabric is off grain when you cut out your pattern, it may pull and pucker, and your finished garment won't hang correctly.

You will find the pattern guide sheet and the tissue pattern pieces inside the pattern envelope. Think of the guide sheet as your instruction book for constructing this garment.

The guide sheet includes:
• **Illustrations** of all the pattern pieces included in the envelope for the different pattern views.
• **An explanation of symbols** and terms used in marking the pattern pieces.
• **A fabric key** to identify the right side, wrong side, interfacing, and lining. These shadings vary among pattern companies.
• **General information** about interfacing, adjusting the pattern, cutting and marking, and sewing.
• **Cutting layouts** that illustrate how to place the pattern pieces on

Straightening Fabric Grain

If you don't think your fabric's grain is straight, here are two ways to straighten the grain.

PULL-A-THREAD METHOD (the preferred method)
1. Clip through the selvage and pull one of the threads. You probably won't need to remove the thread because pulling it slightly creates a small pucker that gives you a guide for cutting.

2. Cut along the pulled-thread line with a rotary cutter or shears. Once you have straightened the fabric using this method, you can make subsequent cuts by measuring from the straight edge and then cutting.

CLIP-AND-TEAR METHOD
This technique usually works best on very lightweight cotton or cotton blend fabrics, such as polyester/cotton batiste. On some fabrics, however, the torn edge flutes excessively. Try this technique on a scrap first to see if it's a suitable method for the fabric you're using.

1. Clip through the selvage and tear across the width of the fabric.

2. Trim the edges with a ruler, rotary cutter, and cutting mat.

the fabric before you cut them out.
• **Step-by-step instructions** and illustrations showing how to make the project from start to finish.

Preparing a Pattern
Unfold the pattern and take out the pieces you need for the view you've selected. If two or more pieces are printed on the same sheet, cut out the pieces you need, leaving a margin of tissue around each piece. You'll trim the excess tissue to the cutting line when you cut out the

garment. Return the other pieces to the pattern envelope.

Press the pattern pieces you need with a warm, dry iron to remove any wrinkles that might distort the shape of the pattern pieces when you cut out the garment. Separate larger pattern pieces from smaller ones.

Familiarize yourself with the different symbols printed on the pattern pieces (*Diagram A*, page 41). Think of them as highway signs—they help you get where you want to go.

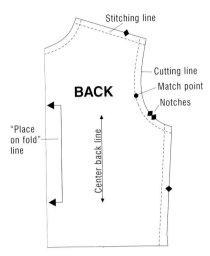

Diagram A: Pattern symbols (notches, arrows) indicate how to use them.

- **Cutting line**—a solid, dark outer line. A pair of scissors is often drawn at intervals on the cutting line.
- **Stitching line**—a broken line drawn ⅝", ⅜", or ¼" inside the cutting line. This is the line on which you will sew.
- **Grain line arrow**—an arrow printed on the pattern piece to help you correctly align the pattern on the fabric. The arrow must lie parallel to the grain (usually lengthwise) of the fabric.
- **"Place on fold" line**—a thinner line than the cutting line, drawn parallel to the edge of the pattern piece. It usually has a double-ended arrow at each end that points to the actual fold line. "Place on fold" is generally printed along the arrow.
- **Notches**—single, double, or triple diamonds. Notches help you match garment pieces accurately when you sew.
- **Match points**—circles and squares that help you match

garment pieces precisely. These marks may indicate points at which to start or stop stitching.
- **Other lines**—special lines, such as hemline, center front, center back, and fold lines, show placement of construction details. "Lengthen or shorten here" lines show recommended positions for adding length to or subtracting it from the pattern without changing the lines or fit of the garment.

Laying Out a Project

The pattern guide sheet shows how to place the pattern pieces on the fabric. You usually have several pattern layouts to choose from. Select the correct layout according to the view you've chosen, your size, and the width of your fabric.

Fold the fabric as indicated on the layout. There are three common ways to position the fabric for layout.
- Both selvages meet at one side. All pieces are cut double. Use this layout for balanced designs.
- Selvages butt in the middle of the fabric, creating two fabric folds (*Diagram B*). Use this layout for patterns that call for both the front

and back pieces to be placed on the fold. You can also use this layout if a center crease in your fabric won't iron out.
- Selvages offset so that part of the fabric is a single thickness. Use this layout for asymmetrical designs, where you need to cut only one of several pieces. To be sure you cut patterns on the grain, measure so that the distance from the selvage to the fold is the same thoughout the layout.

Following the instructions in the guide sheet, lay out the larger pattern pieces along the grain line of the fabric. Measure the distance from both ends of the printed grain line arrow to the fabric fold. These measurements should be the same. Then make sure both ends of the arrow measure the same distance from the selvage (*Diagram C*, page 42). Pin the pattern to the fabric at each end of the arrow to hold it in place as you lay out the remaining pieces.

If a pattern piece has a "place on

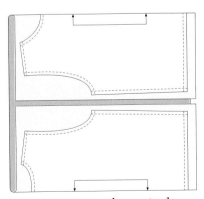

Diagram B: Butt selvages in the middle to avoid a center crease or when both front and back must be cut on the fold.

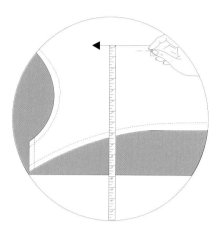

Diagram C: Measure from grain arrow to selvage.

fold" line, be sure to place the line **exactly** on the fabric fold. Pin the pattern to the fabric along the fold line, with pins at right angles to the fold. Extend the heads of the pins over the edge of the fold; this will remind you not to cut into the fold by mistake.

To pin smaller pattern pieces to the fabric, position the pattern piece on the fabric. Place a pin diagonally in each corner (*Diagram D*). Pin from corner to corner, placing the pins parallel to the cutting line (but not on the line), every 6" to 8". Use extra pins around curved areas and on smaller pieces.

Knit Layout

Most knits have a crease in the center of the fabric as they come off the bolt. Sometimes it's hard to remove that crease, and you certainly don't want it showing down the center of your finished garment. Because most knit fabrics are 60" wide, you can easily reposition the crease and still have plenty of room for laying out pattern pieces. Here are some tips that simplify laying out and cutting knit fabrics.

1. Refold the fabric so selvage ends meet in the center of the knit fabric. This eliminates having a crease fall within the body of the garment and provides adequate width for positioning most front and back pattern pieces.

2. Use a "With Nap" layout.

> ### Note from Nancy
>
> A "With Nap" layout means that the tops of all pattern pieces must face in the same direction. Using a With Nap layout for knits prevents shading or having the finished garment appear to be of two different colors.

3. If some pattern pieces, such as sleeves, do not fit on the refolded fabric, position and cut the larger pieces, such as the front and back, first. Then refold the fabric to cut the smaller pieces.

4. Save layout time by using pattern weights.

• Begin by pinning one end of the grain line arrow on each pattern piece. (See instructions beginning on page 40.)

• Use weights to secure the remaining pattern edges. Position the weights near the edges of one piece and cut it out. Then move the weights to another piece; cut. Repeat until you cut all pieces (*Diagram E*).

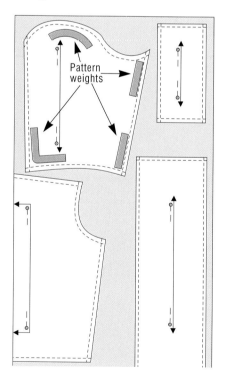

Diagram E: Use pattern weights to secure pattern pieces.

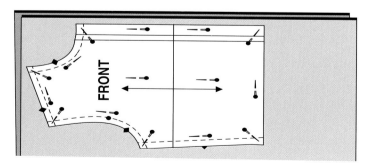

Diagram D: Pin the pattern diagonally at the corners.

Specialty Fabric Layout

When you're working with specialty fabric, such as Ultrasuede, it's smart to make a test layout before buying fabric. Doing so usually saves fabric—and money!

If you're planning to sew with heavily napped fabric that requires cutting in single fabric layers, cut a complete pattern for each section. Use waxed paper to make a reverse of separate pattern pieces (a left or right back, for example, to go with the one printed) or to make a complete pattern piece that is marked to cut on a fold. Be sure you're using a mirror image pattern for garment pieces that need both left and right versions. Otherwise, you may end up with two left arms or two right fronts.

Lay out the pattern pieces on a single layer of 45"-wide checked or plaid fabric. Because Ultrasuede is also 45" wide, this will give you a fairly accurate indication of how much fabric you will need. Using a checked or plaid fabric makes it easy to check the grain line.

Place the main pattern pieces (front and back) on the straight grain.

Use a one-way napped layout with all pattern pieces facing in the same direction.

If you're using Ultrasuede, you may position facing pieces slightly off grain to economize on fabric. Grain line can shift up to 45° on facing pieces without noticeable change in the shade of the suede.

After positioning all pattern pieces, measure the length of fabric needed, and compare this measurement to the yardage listed on the pattern envelope.

Measuring Tools

For clothes to fit, quilts to go together without bunching, and home decorating projects to cover surfaces, you must measure carefully when you cut. See page 148 for a list of measuring tools with photographs .

• A **curved ruler**, such as the Fashion Ruler, helps you mark French curves, alterations to hiplines or princess seams, and other shaped seam lines.

• **Quilting rulers** are heavy-duty, clear acrylic rulers, developed for quilters to use with rotary cutters. They're also useful in other sewing projects. See page 44 for information on using a rotary cutter and quilting ruler to cut garment pieces. Quilting rulers come in various sizes, as well as in triangles and squares. Commonly used sizes are listed below.

A 1" x 6" pocket-size ruler is convenient and versatile for quilting and sewing.

Keep a 1" x 12½" ruler next to your sewing machine for quick measuring references.

The larger 3" x 18" ruler is great for secondary cutting and for fine patchwork techniques. Use positions clearly marked on the ruler to cut accurate 30°, 45°, and 60° angles.

• A 6" **sewing gauge** has a double-pointed slide to mark hems, tucks, pleats, buttons, and buttonhole placements. Many sewing gauges are also marked in centimeters.

• A **tape measure** is an essential sewing tool. Usually 60" long (152 cm), these flexible rulers are so handy, many sewers keep them in both their purses and their sewing boxes.

Using the right tools for marking your pattern (page 46) makes sewing easier.

Cutting Time-Savers

When you're ready to cut out your fabric pieces, streamline your cutting sessions by following these timesaving strategies:

• **Use sharp shears, cutting with long, smooth strokes.** For best results, use 8" dressmaker shears for cutting fabrics. Sharpen the shears periodically to ensure clean-cut edges. Use a sharpening stone to hone cutting edges and to prevent dull spots. Reserve these shears for cutting only fabric.

Note from Nancy

Readers and viewers often ask me to explain the difference between scissors and shears. Shears, perfect for cutting out fabric, are more than 6" long. They have different handle bows or loops, one to fit the thumb and a larger one to fit two or more fingers. Scissors, perfect for trimming, snipping, and crafting, are shorter than 6" and have identical finger and thumb bows. A little sewing trivia can help when buying or choosing the right cutting tool.

• **Move around the fabric** rather than moving the fabric toward you.
• **Cut notches even with the cutting line** rather than cutting around the diamond shapes. This gives a smoother line. You can mark the notches later.
• **If your pattern calls for interfacing, cut out the interfacing at the same time** you cut out the rest of the project.
• **Cut two layers at the same time.** If you're making a lined skirt, stack the skirt and lining fabrics and cut out both at once. Or cut two blouses at the same time. Here are guidelines for stacking fabrics:
1. The fabrics must be the same width.
2. The fabrics should be no heavier than medium weight. Heavier fabrics, when stacked, are too bulky to cut easily and accurately.
3. Pin the two fabric layers together along the fold and the selvages before laying out the pattern.
4. Place slippery fabrics on top.
5. You cannot stack fabrics that require matching, such as plaids and stripes.
• **Use pattern weights.** Pattern weights save time by reducing the number of pins you need. They come in many shapes and sizes. Some are round washerlike weights; some are shaped to fit pattern angles and curves; still others are molded in the shape of sewing paraphernalia. See page 42 for instructions on using pattern weights.
• **Use adjoining cutting lines.** Whenever possible, place straight cutting lines adjacent to each other (*Diagram A*). You'll make one cut for both lines. For example, you can cut the lower edge of a top and the upper edge of a cuff simultaneously. Be sure grain lines correspond.
• **Use a rotary cutter, cutting mat, and ruler.** Rotary cutters,

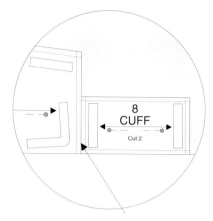

Diagram A: Butt patterns at straight cutting lines.

cutting mats, and gridded rulers have changed the way home sewers, fabric crafters, and quilters cut fabric. In seconds, a rotary cutter, used in combination with a cutting mat and ruler, can slice through several layers of fabric accurately.

Rotary cutters are available in two sizes. The heavy-duty model used by most quilters has a blade with a 2¾" (45 mm) diameter. The smaller size has a blade with a 1⅛" (28 mm) diameter.

Use the smaller cutter to cut out pattern pieces on light- to midweight fabrics; it provides greater maneuverability around curved areas than the larger size. Save the larger cutter for straight pieces or heavier fabrics. You'll be amazed at how much time you save when cutting out smaller pattern pieces, such as interfacings, ribbings, and children's garments.

When cutting with a rotary cutter, using a gridded cutting mat is a must. The mat is made of a special "self-healing" material the cutting blade doesn't damage. It also protects the surface of your work table. Look for rectangular sizes from 6" x 18" up to 36" x 48". Larger mats are easier to work with, so it's a good idea to buy the largest size you can afford.

The third essential rotary-cutting tool is a ruler. Transparent, gridded Plexiglass rulers, made especially for use with rotary cutters, are available in a wide variety of sizes, ranging from a 4" x 4" square to a 6" x 24" rectangle.

Cutting Tools

Cutting tools traditionally centered on shears and scissors. But rotary cutters and mats aren't the only innovations you'll find in this area of notions. Other cutting tools my staff and I use are listed below. See page 140 for a list with photographs of these tools.

• Use **appliqué scissors** for trimming close to edgestitching. The scissors' large bill lifts the fabric to be trimmed, and the curved handles ensure a comfortable hand position.

• A **buttonhole cutter and block** helps you make neat, professional-looking buttonholes. The cutter has a hardwood handle with a hardened steel blade; the block comes in various shapes. Place the buttonhole over the block and cut with the cutter. If the buttonhole is smaller than the cutter, place half the buttonhole over the edge of the block, cut, and repeat for the second part.

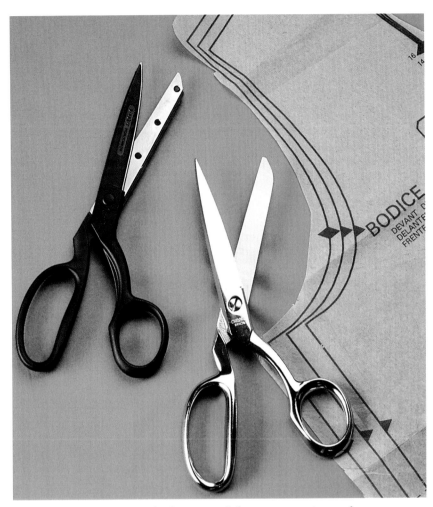

Keeping your cutting tools sharp simplifies many sewing tasks.

• Handy **buttonhole scissors** allow you to make precise buttonhole cuts. Adjust the screw at the handle of the scissors to hold them partially open. This allows you to use part of the blade to make precise ½" to 1¼" (1.3 cm to 3.8 cm) buttonhole cuts. Fabric in front of the buttonhole bunches safely in a reservoir at the base of the blade.

• **Pinking shears** have sawtooth edges to create decorative, ravel-resistant finishes for seams and trim. When you trim curved seam allowances with pinking shears, you automatically reduce bulk in the finished seam.

• The **Gingher sharpening stone**, while not actually a cutting tool, is useful for maintaining your sewing shears and scissors. Work along the beveled surface of the knife edge blade, sliding the stone upward, working from the tip of the blade to the shank. After honing, wipe the blade clean.

If your pattern is the road map for your project, the notches, matching points, and other pattern details are the street signs. Once you've cut out all pattern pieces, you must mark these details carefully and accurately in order to assemble your garment efficiently.

These pattern details include:
• **Notches**
• **Hemlines**
• **Darts and pleats**
• **Center front and center back lines**
• **Dots, squares, and button and pocket placements**

Generally, mark all pattern details on the wrong side of the fabric. If you have a hard time distinguishing the right side from the wrong side, indicate the right side by marking within the seam allowance using chalk or a water-soluble marking pen.

If you cut two layers at the same time, be sure to mark both layers.

When I learned to sew, I marked details using tracing paper and a tracing wheel. This method is still popular, but you can speed up and simplify the task by combining other marking methods. See page 147 for a chart of marking tools.

Clip Marking

Clip (nip) notches instead of cutting them outward (*Diagram*). Make ¼" (6 mm) straight nips into seam allowances. Be careful not to clip deeper than ¼" (6 mm), or you'll reduce your seam width. Always plan for maximum seam-allowance width, in case you must make alterations after the first fitting.

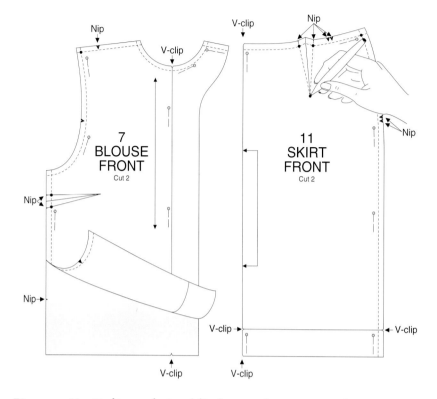

Diagram: Use V-clips and nips (clips) to mark pattern notches.

• Clip-mark ends of darts within the seam allowance. Use chalk or a water-soluble marking pen to mark the points of darts. Do not clip dart points!
• Clip to indicate garment hemlines, making a ¼" (6 mm) clip in each side at the seam allowance.

V-Clip Marking

V-clips are similar to straight clips except that you remove a small V-shaped section of fabric.
• Use V-clips to indicate center backs and fronts on garment, collars, and facings.
• Make V-clips ¼" to ⅜" (6 mm to 9 mm) deep. If the center front or center back is on the fold, simply angle-cut along the fold; when you open the piece flat, you'll see that a V shape has formed.

Pen/Pencil and Chalk Marking

Use water- or air-soluble marking pens or pencils, chalk, or chalk wheels for marking darts, pleats, buttonhole and button placements, and circle or dot pattern markings. Mark on the wrong side of the fabric.

To use a pen, pencil, or chalk, follow this procedure:
1. Poke a pin through each pattern dot or marking you need to transfer.
2. Carefully remove the pattern from the fabric. Start at the outside pattern edges and work toward the center, pulling the pins gently through the pattern piece.
3. Mark each pin's position using the marker. If you cut two layers of

fabric at the same time, mark the wrong side of each layer.

After sewing, use a drop of water to remove washable markings. Air-soluble pens make purple marks that vanish without washing in 12 to 24 hours.

Tracing Wheel and Tracing Paper

Here's how to transfer markings using a tracing wheel and tracing paper.
• Use the lightest color sewing tracing paper that will show on your fabric. This is important, because tracing paper marks are sometimes hard to remove.
• Place the colored side of the tracing paper next to the wrong side of each fabric piece.
• Protect the table by placing cardboard under the fabric. The wheel's sharp points damage some surfaces.
• Run the tracing wheel along the pattern markings. To make tracing straight lines easier, use a ruler as a guide. Press firmly so that markings show on both layers. Test a fabric scrap before marking your project so that you know how hard to press.
• After marking one area, reposition tracing paper and cardboard. Continue

until you transfer all markings.

Marks for Serging

For seams that I plan to serge, I transfer pattern markings to the wrong side of the fabric (along the seam line, if possible) using a water-soluble marking pen. Clip markings aren't suitable for serger construction. If you cut garment pieces using standard $5/8''$ seam allowances, the serger would trim away clip markings as you stitch. And if you cut the pieces using a $1/4''$ (6 mm) seam allowance, clip markings would weaken the seam.

Marking Knits

Although clipping is a timesaving way to mark details on patterns, knit patterns often allow only $1/4''$ (6 mm) seam allowances. Clipping into that narrow area could weaken a seam. Try one or both of these alternatives.
• Use a fabric marking pen.
• Use Pattern Pals (see at right) to transfer pattern details.

Marking Tools

The following tools help ensure that your sewing is accurate.
• **Chalk** is an oil-free marking tool, which is available in several forms.

A *chalk wheel* accurately transfers markings to fabric with a fine line of chalk. Fill the wheel with loose white chalk (for dark fabrics) or blue chalk (for light fabrics).

Triangle Tailor's Chalk has a chalk base in a firm triangular form. It comes in red, yellow, white, and blue, and it never leaves a stain.

A *Soapstone Fabric Marker,* made from natural soapstone, creates marks that are clearly visible, yet rub off easily when no longer needed. Use a pencil sharpener to sharpen this adjustable tool. The Soapstone Fabric Marker does not show up on light-colored fabrics.
• A **pinpoint fabric marking pen** draws fine lines. Fabric marking pens are available in air- and water-soluble form.
• The **Wonder Marker**'s blue ink disappears with just a drop of water.
• A **fabric marking pencil** has a super-thin lead specifically designed for fabric. Since it contains less graphite than a standard pencil, it resists smearing and washes out.
• A **permanent fabric marker** is ideal for drawing embellishment details on garments, but don't use it for marking pattern details. The marks dry quickly and will not fade, smear, or feather when dry. The ink is also waterproof.
• **Pattern Pals** are pressure-sensitive symbols that make transferring pattern details to fabric easy. They are ideal for marking notches, dots, and circles on seams that you will serge because they eliminate the need for nips.
• **Pattern transfer materials** include the traditional saw-toothed tracing wheel and tracing or transfer paper. The paper is reusable, wax-free, and carbonless, and marks erase, sponge off, or wash out. The paper comes in a variety of colors.

PREPARING TO SEW

Once you've cut out your pattern, the next steps are to choose the right needle and thread and set up your machine. Sewing will be easier and faster if you also have a few handy notions. • **Needles come in a variety of sizes** for sewing by hand or by machine. And you can buy thread in a dazzling array of colors. Some threads even have special finishes, such as metallic or shiny rayon layers, that accent garments beautifully. Clear monofilament thread makes almost invisible stitches. • **Machine setup is easy,** with only a few changes necessary to prepare for specialty sewing, such as machine embroidery.

Until the mid-nineteenth century, needles were made by hand, so they were expensive and somewhat rare. A family from that era sometimes owned only one needle. Now, the problem isn't keeping up with your family's only needle—it's choosing the right one!

Note from Nancy

Think of the number of times the sewing machine needle must pierce the fabric for each project, and you'll realize why the point of the needle quickly becomes dull or develops a burr. The result? Pulled or snagged threads in your fabric, or skipped stitches. If you haven't made it a practice already, eliminate these avoidable sewing problems by changing your needle frequently. I recommend changing the needle with each new sewing project. If your serger also uses regular sewing machine needles, change its needles with each serging project, too.

You can use universal-point needles on both knit and woven fabrics.

Sewing Machine Needles

Sewing machine needles are sold in a variety of sizes and types. The shape of the point differs from type to type, the shape and size of the eye may also change, and the needle thickness varies, too.

Choose the size and type that's appropriate for both the fabric and thread you're using and the type of sewing you plan to do. See the chart on page 149 for a list of needles and appropriate uses.

A sewing machine needle has a shank, a shaft, a scarf, an eye, and a point (*Diagram*). The shank fits into your machine's needle holder, and it has a rounded side and a flat side. The indentation behind the eye is called the scarf, which helps ensure proper stitch formation. The needle groove is on the same side as the rounded part of the shaft. It supports the thread as the needle goes in and out of the fabric.

Higher numbers identify larger sewing machine needles. For example, a size 110 denim needle is larger than a size 90 denim needle. Generally, the larger the needle, the heavier the fabric for which it's appropriate. Use smaller sizes with more delicate fabrics and larger sizes with heavier fabrics.

The eye of the needle varies depending on the type of needle. Needles specially designed for sewing with metallic and decorative threads (**metallic and machine embroidery needles**) have longer eyes than those of **universal needles**. They are designed this way to accommodate thicker threads without causing them to break or fray.

Point shape also varies. The point on a **universal needle** is a blend of sharp and ballpoint, making it suitable for many types of fabric. A **stretch needle** has a ballpoint that slides between the threads of knit or elastic fabrics. The point on a **leather needle** is wedge-shaped to reduce the chance that the needle hole will tear. **Microtex needles** have very sharp points at the end of slender shafts to pierce dense microfibers, such as Ultrasuede and tencel.

Use a size 70 or 80 universal needle to stitch medium-weight woven fabrics, and use a size 75 stretch needle to stitch lightweight knits. Don't hesitate to change needle size if your test stitching shows that the needle in your machine makes too large a hole or if your machine skips stitches.

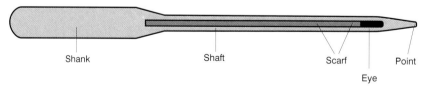

Shank   Shaft   Scarf   Point   Eye

Diagram: Sewing machine needles have several parts. The shank has a flat side and a rounded side. The scarf is an indentation behind the eye. The point may be sharp or rounded to go through knits without damaging the fibers.

Specialty Machine Needles

Some sewing machine needles are designed for special purposes. A **wing needle** has wide, wing-shaped blades on either side to make a hole that resembles entre-deux trim. A **spring needle** has an attached spring that holds down the fabric while you do free-motion embroidery or quilting. A **top-stitching needle** has a large eye to accommodate buttonhole twist or other decorative thread.

Double needles are probably the most popular of all specialty needles, because they produce perfectly parallel rows of stitching every time. Double needles (sometimes called twin needles) fit any zigzag machine that threads from front to back. Because the needles are fixed a certain distance apart, the lines of parallel stitching are sewn simultaneously, and the distance between the two rows never changes. Use double-needle topstitching to add a tailored accent to casual clothes. It also makes an attractive finish on the hems of knit garments.

Double needles come in a variety of sizes from 1.6 mm to 8.0 mm. The numbers indicate the amount of space between the needles. Sometimes double needle sizes are listed with two numbers, such as 4.0/100. In this case, the first number refers to the distance in millimeters between the two needles, and the second number represents the size of each needle.

You can also buy **triple needles**, which form three parallel rows of stitching at once.

Hand-Sewing Needles

Hand-sewing needles also come in a variety of sizes and types that are geared for different types of sewing. Unlike machine needles, hand-sewing needles use larger numbers to indicate shorter and finer needles. For instance, a size 3 sharp (a type of needle) is much

larger than a size 10 sharp. Choose the smallest needle (which means a higher number) that will go through your fabric without bending or breaking.

Sharps are the most commonly used general-purpose hand-sewing needles. They have round eyes and sharp points and are of medium length.

Betweens are shorter than sharps, which makes them popular with quilters. The shorter length makes it easier to take fine stitches through

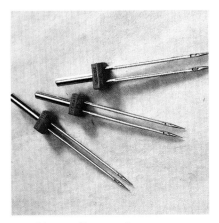

Double needles are the most frequently used specialty needles.

Different machine stitches require different needles. Shown from left are: topstitching, metallic, embroidery, double stretch, double 4.0, double 2.0, double 3.0, double 1.6, and all-purpose.

several layers of fabric and batting.

Ballpoint needles are like sharps, except they have rounded points. Use a ballpoint needle to sew knits—the round point pushes between fabric yarns instead of piercing them.

Crewel needles have long eyes that make them easier to thread than sharps. The eye also accommodates several strands of floss or thread for decorative handwork such as embroidery.

Tapestry needles have blunt tips and are larger than general-purpose hand-sewing needles. They are primarily designed for crafts such as needlepoint. Use a tapestry needle as a bodkin to thread thin ribbon or other decorative thread through eyelet trim or to anchor thread ends of a serged seam under the stitching.

Double-eyed needles have blunt tips with eyes on each end that are useful for weaving threads or trim underneath stitches. Keep the ends of serged seams neat and secure by inserting the thread ends into either of the needle's eyes and threading the needle under the stitches of the seam. Pull the needle through, anchoring the thread ends so that they won't unravel.

Just as with machine needles, there are hand-sewing needles for special purposes, such as heavy-duty sewing, beading, darning, and weaving. You can even find curved needles, some with points on both ends, for use in upholstery and rugmaking.

Straight Pins

These essential sewing tools are categorized by the length of the pin and the type of head. Like needles, they are inexpensive, so keep plenty on hand. Avoid using pins that are bent or have burrs.

Pins vary both in length and in thickness or diameter. Most pins are .5 mm or .6 mm thick, but you can buy thicker pins for special purposes.

Silk pins have flat heads and are suitable in length and diameter for general dressmaking uses. They are also called dressmaker's pins.

Quilting pins or **general-purpose pins** are longer and slightly thicker than silk pins, making them useful for pinning heavier fabrics and multiple layers of fabric.

Appliqué pins are shorter and thinner than silk pins. They are especially useful for pinning small pieces together or for pinning tight corners.

Flower head pins are extra long and have flat, colored heads that make them easy to pick up and to locate in your fabric.

Glass or plastic head pins are slightly shorter than flower head pins. Like flower head pins, they are easier to see than flat head pins. Be sure to remove all plastic head pins before pressing your project, because the heat of the iron may melt the plastic head.

T-pins are usually longer than silk pins and have a T-shaped head. They're useful for pinning loose knits and for upholstery and other craft projects.

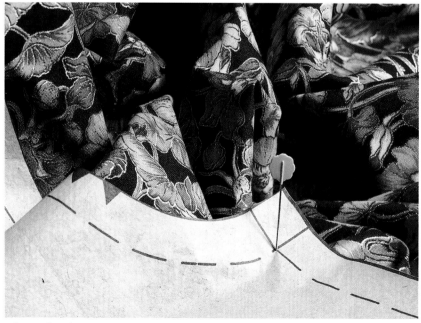

Flower head pins are easy to locate, especially in textured or printed fabrics.

Storage

Store needles and pins in stuffed pincushions or in magnetic pin holders.

The most popular **stuffed pincushion** is tomato-shaped, but you can make your own or buy other kinds. If you make your own, use wool for stuffing rather than cotton. Wool has more loft, body, and resilience than cotton, and you can pack wool tighter inside the pincushion.

Magnetic pin holders come in a variety of shapes and sizes, including ones you can wear on your wrist while sewing. They are handy for picking up dropped pins and needles. A word of caution: If you have a computerized sewing machine, never place a magnetic pin holder directly on the machine, because the magnet may erase some of the machine's computer data.

Magnetic pin holders have become popular, but they should be kept off computerized sewing machines.

You can also store needles in airtight needle cases, or save the packages they came in to store slightly used ones.

Never leave pins or needles in fabric, because they can rust and stain the fabric. To minimize rusting, remember to keep your pincushions or pin holders away from damp places.

Don't sew over a pin, or, if you must, move the flywheel slowly by hand until you're safely past it. If the machine needle hits a pin, it can bend or break the needle.

Keep pins and needles out of your mouth.

Clean needles and pins by passing them through an emery bag.

Many tomato pincushions have strawberry-shaped emery bags attached to them. If you prefer magnetic pin holders, buy a separate strawberry emery bag. Using an emery bag to clean your pins and needles can lengthen their usefulness, but it won't remove rust or serious burrs.

thread CHOICES

For successful sewing, there's more to choosing thread than just picking the right color. You also need the right weight and type of thread for your fabric and for the kind of sewing that you're doing. See the chart beginning on page 155 for details on types of thread.

Choose thread the same color or one shade darker than your fashion fabric. Thread appears lighter after it's sewn than it does on the spool. When working with prints, tweeds, or plaids, match thread to the predominant or background color.

If your stitches aren't smooth and uniform, check your sewing machine needle for damage, and be sure it's the correct size and type. The needle should match the thread type, the fabric, and the sewing technique (see page 50).

Size

Thread is generally described by two numbers, the weight and the ply. For example, all-purpose thread is 50/3, which means that its weight is 50 and it's made of three plies (or strands) of thread twisted together. The larger the weight number, the finer the thread. For example, an 80/2 cotton thread is very fine and suitable for heirloom sewing, while a 40/3 buttonhole twist is a thick, heavy thread suitable for topstitching.

All-purpose sewing thread is three-ply, but the thread you use on a serger is two-ply. Because sergers stitch with more threads than conventional sewing machines—usually three to five, depending on the type of seam—they need lighter-weight thread to reduce bulk at the seam line.

For most types of sewing, use all-purpose thread made of cotton-covered polyester or 100% polyester.

Specialty Threads

Specialty threads are made in several weights and from different fibers to suit many purposes. See the chart beginning on page 155 for information on types of thread available.

Note from Nancy

I don't recommend using serger thread, which is usually lighter than conventional sewing thread, on your sewing machine. However, you can use conventional sewing thread in a serger.

If you use sewing machine thread in your serger, put a serger cap over each thread spool. Sewing machine thread is wound to feed off the side of the spool, but serger thread feeds off the top. The serger cap fits in the top opening of the spool, preventing the thread from catching on the slit in the rim of the spool.

Monofilament thread blends readily with most fabrics and is nearly invisible on the right side of a completed hem. Available in clear and smoke tint, this thread is made of nylon and is very heat sensitive. When pressing a project, you must use a press cloth to cover any

Thread comes in a rainbow of colors, as well as a wide range of types and weights.

seams stitched with this thread.

Elastic thread isn't really thread; it's a dense strand of spun elastic. Elastic thread is too thick to pass through the eye of a machine needle, but you can zigzag or serge over it to stabilize a shoulder seam. Hand-wind the elastic thread in the bobbin; when you stitch, the elastic will gather the fabric, creating the look of smocking.

Rayon embroidery threads with luster and sheen are almost synonymous with machine embroidery. Look for the popular 40 weight in a wide range of colors, or the 30 weight (a heavier thread) in a more limited offering.

Cotton embroidery thread has a matte finish that gives machine embroidery work a softer, heirloom look.

Decorative and embellishment threads and yarns are made from cotton, wool, silk, linen, acrylic, or blends. Use these threads for surface embellishment such as couching.

Coned serger thread comes in a wide variety of colors. If you have trouble matching thread color to your fabric, try using sewing machine thread for the needles in your serger and neutral-colored thread for the upper and lower loopers. Because the looper threads don't show from the right side of the finished garment, they don't have to match the fabric color exactly. Even though regular sewing machine thread is heavier than serger thread, using it in the needle won't noticeably increase the weight of

the seam, because the needle thread forms only one line of stitching.

Metallic threads beautifully accent dressy garments and accessories. Whether you're sewing or serging, you can use this shimmery thread to topstitch, couch, flatlock, or add other embellishments. Because of its metal content (metallic thread usually has a foil-wrapped core), this thread may be a bit wiry and much more brittle than all-purpose thread. Handle it carefully when threading. Use a needle designed for metallic threads, and loosen the tension as needed to prevent the thread from breaking and to keep the stitches smooth and even.

Note from Nancy

When I serge using metallic thread, I like to blend it with texturized nylon, serger, or all-purpose thread. This enhances the color, durability, and coverage of the metallic thread. To blend these threads, I combine two threads in the looper and treat them as one. I place the additional spool or cone on a thread stand behind the machine. Then I adjust the tensions so that the threads feed uniformly.

Bobbin thread is ideal to wind on the bobbin when using decorative (metallic or machine embroidery) threads on top of the machine. The lightweight nylon thread will not add bulk or weight to embroidery,

monogramming, or pintucks. You can buy convenient prewound bobbins for creative work. These cardboard bobbins or bobbinless (compressed) thread save time, allowing you more time to sew!

Texturized nylon thread, such as woolly nylon, is a multifilament, crimped thread. It has more stretch than either serger or all-purpose thread. Use it when serging lingerie, baby clothes, swimwear, and leotards to make the most of its softness. Because texturized nylon thread is crimped, it provides more coverage for narrow rolled-edge and decorative serging. When you use this thread, you may need to loosen the needle or looper tension slightly.

ThreadFuse is a polyester thread twisted with a heat-activated fusible fiber. ThreadFuse bonds to fabric like magic with just the touch of a steam iron.

Match thread to fabric for invisible seams, or use a contrasting color to accent a project.

Every sewing machine and serger is different in the features it offers and in the way you set it up. **Read your owner's manual and keep it handy for easy reference.** The manual is a great resource for learning how to thread and adjust the machine and how to wind and thread the bobbin.

Changing Needles

Inserting a new needle in the machine for each project helps prevent skipped stitches. Insert the needle so that the flat portion of the shank is at the back and you can see through the eye of the needle. Check your owner's manual if you're not sure how to insert the needle.

If your serger uses regular sewing machine needles, change the needles with each project. If it uses industrial needles, change them after every two to three projects.

Note from Nancy

Use a needle inserter to help you change the needles in your machine. The inserter firmly holds the needle in a specially tapered hole while you tighten the needle screw. This tool is just 3¼" long, and it fits where your finger won't! Use it for changing both sewing machine and serger needles.

Threading the Machine

A sewing machine uses a spool of thread on top of the machine for the upper thread supply and a bobbin filled with thread for the lower thread supply. A serger uses separate cones of thread for each of the loopers and the needle(s). Check your owner's manual to learn how to thread your machine and wind the bobbin.

Note from Nancy

"Floss" your sewing machine whenever you thread it to remove built-up lint. To do this, clip the thread at the spool and pull it out through the needle.

The owner's manual tells you what kind of bobbin your sewing machine uses. Bobbins are inexpensive, so keep extras on hand. Before you start a big project, wind two or more bobbins so that you don't have to stop in the middle of a seam, unthread your machine, and wind a fresh bobbin.

Changing threads on a serger can seem like a daunting task if you've never done it before. To make it a snap, don't remove previous threads from the machine. Instead, try this method:
1. Clip the threads near the thread spools. Remove the spools and replace them with new ones.
2. Tie new threads to the old threads using a square knot (*Diagram A*). Tug on each knot to make sure it's secure. If it isn't, retie the knot and test it until it's secure. Clip the thread tails close to the knot.
3. Lift the presser foot and raise the needle. Write down the tension settings so that you can return the dials to the correct settings after you change threads. Now loosen all tensions to 0 or to minus numbers.
4. Pull the threads through the machine.
   • Pull the needle thread through the machine. Cut each thread at the needle, clipping off the knot joining the old thread to the new thread. If you have more than one needle, pull both threads through at the same time (*Diagram B*).
   • Next, pull the threads for the lower and upper loopers through the machine (*Diagram C*).
   • Rethread the needle(s).
5. Pull all the threads to the left under the presser foot, and return the tensions to their original settings. Hold the threads and press the foot control until a thread chain forms (*Diagram D*).

If you can't find the color serger thread you want, or if you have a small project to serge, use thread wound onto sewing machine bobbins. Simply place them on the cone thread holders, and thread the machine as usual.

Note from Nancy

Two serger notions that I find extremely helpful are serger tweezers and a serger threader. I use the tweezers when rethreading the needles and the serger threader for rethreading the loopers, if they come undone. Look for serger tools that are extra long to get into those hard-to-reach areas.

Rethreading a Serger

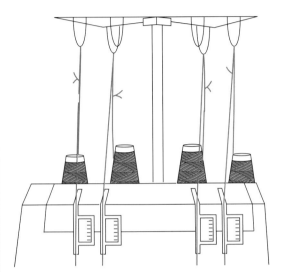

Diagram A: Tie new threads to old threads with a square knot.

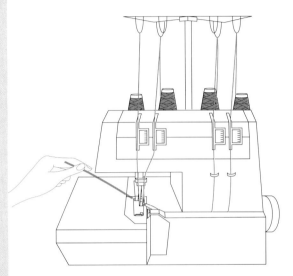

Diagram B: Pull needle thread through machine.

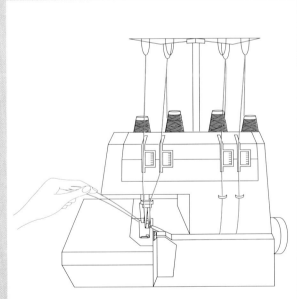

Diagram C: Pull threads through upper and lower loopers.

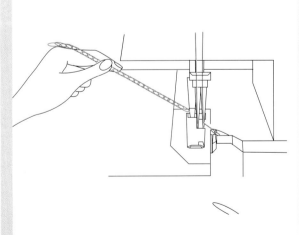

Diagram D: Make a thread chain and pull it through serger.

Basic Tension Settings

For most seaming, your stitches should be balanced. That means that the seam will look the same from both the right and the wrong sides. That's true whether you're sewing a straightstitch or a zigzag stitch, or if you're serging an over-lock seam.

On a **sewing machine,** bobbin tension is almost always preset by the manufacturer. Most machines have a tension regulator dial for controlling the tightness of the upper thread. Check the owner's manual for correct settings. When you test-stitch on scraps of your project fabric, you may find that you need to adjust the upper ten-sion in order to get smooth, even stitches. (See page 62 for details on stitching a perfect seam.)

On a **serger,** manufacturers set the tensions for a balanced over-lock stitch. Some brands mark the tension disks or dials with an *N* for normal (balanced). An overlock stitch is balanced when the stitch looks the same from both the right and wrong sides. Also, the threads from the two loops should inter-lock with the needle thread on the left, and with each other at the fab-ric edge on the right. The needle thread should hug the fabric and secure the looper threads without forming loops or causing puckers. (See page 66 for details on serging the perfect seam.)

Note from Nancy

Here's an easy way to trouble-shoot serger tension problems and to better understand the position of each thread within the stitch. Practice with a different-colored thread in each needle and looper. You'll easily recognize which thread requires tension adjustment. If the overlock stitch isn't balanced, begin by loosening the looper that's too tight. Adjust the looper tensions first. If you don't see enough of the thread, loosen the tension; if you see too much thread (excess loops), tighten the tension.

Having trouble remembering which way to turn your tension disks or dials? My friend Gail Brown, a serger expert, relies on the phrase "righty-tighty and lefty-loosey" for tension disks. For drop-in tension dials, remember "up-tight, down-loose." When in doubt, refer to your owner's manual.

Specialty Setup

If you're planning to sew with a specialty thread, machine setup is only a little different than it is for regular stitching.

To set up your machine to sew with specialty thread:

1. Make sure you've chosen and inserted the correct sewing machine needle and foot. For example, if you're sewing with metallic thread, replace your machine needle with a metallic needle.

2. Wind a bobbin according to the instructions in your sewing machine manual. Choose regular sewing thread for the bobbin that matches your fabric.

3. Thread your machine accord-ing to the instructions in your owner's manual.

4. Sew a test strip, adjusting the tension as needed. For machine embroidery, you usually need to loosen the upper needle tension by two settings. When sewing a test strip, be sure to use the same fabric thicknesses and stabilizers you plan to use for your project.

For example, if you're adding decorative stitching to a blouse front that's only a single fabric thickness, test your stitches on one layer of fabric (plus stabilizer). If you're stitching around button-holes using metallic thread, be sure your test sample has the same number of fabric layers as your buttonhole placket, plus any inter-facing, plus stabilizer.

Always sew test strips. The time you spend on this important step can prevent frustration and save you time in the long run.

SPECIALIZED notions

The term *notions* covers almost any accessory in sewing. The notions category on the back of a pattern envelope usually includes thread, zippers, and other items essential to completing the sewing project. In addition to these basics, specialty notions can streamline the sewing process and save you time.

This section includes information on some of my favorite specialty notions. See page 152 for a chart of these and other notions. Manufacturers introduce notions almost weekly, so be sure to check your local sewing center or your favorite notions catalog for the latest in these timesaving tools.

Bamboo Pointer & Creaser: Brand name for a tool that has a pointed end for turning collars, cuffs, lapels, or appliqués, and a curved, beveled end for temporarily pressing seams open.

Bias tape maker: A metal device that lets you create single-fold bias tape with edges that are always uniform. Slip a bias strip into the wide end of this tool, and pull the strip out the other end as you press. Available in a wide range of widths, from ¼" (6 mm) to 2" (48 mm).

Bodkin: A tweezerlike notion with special teeth used to draw lace, elastic, or ribbon through a casing. You can also use it for weaving.

Little Wooden Iron: Brand name for a unique finger-pressing notion. This smoothly sanded hardwood tool is useful for opening seams and for pressing seams to the side when quilting. Choose a right- or left-handed iron, since the tool's pressing edge is made at an angle.

Seam sealant: A clear-drying liquid that reinforces and locks threads to prevent frayed seams. You can also use it to stabilize buttonholes. Brand names include Fray Check and No-Fray.

The Little Wooden Iron is a handy notion for finger pressing.

Serger looper threader: A tool that helps draw threads through the loopers on a serger. It has a slender wire with a loop at one end and a plastic handle at the other.

Sewing machine cone thread stand: A plastic tool that allows you to use economical cone thread on your sewing machine.

Stiletto: An awl-like tool used to ease fabric, lace, or ribbon under the presser foot as you sew or quilt. Use it to help position seam allowances as you stitch, straighten silk ribbon embroidery stitches, and turn appliqué points.

Thread palette: A device that fits over a serger spool holder or a sewing machine cone thread stand to let you feed as many as five spools of thread into your sewing machine or serger at once. This expands the number of thread colors you can use when sewing or serging decorative stitches.

Trolley Needle Thread Controller: Brand name for a thimble-like device that helps ease seams and ruffles under the presser foot. It's also useful for positioning ribbon, sequins, and other trims while you stitch.

Tube turner: A tool that makes it easier to turn fabric tubes right side out. Available in an assortment of designs and price ranges. Three types are:

• *Collar Point & Tube Turner:* Brand name for a scissorlike tool that turns collar points and pocket flaps. It's also useful for turning spaghetti straps, belts, and other tubes.

• *Fasturn:* Brand name for a tube turner that consists of a metal cylinder and a wire hook. Slip a fabric tube over the cylinder, and use the hook to pull fabric through the inside of the cylinder, turning the tube right side out.

• *Narrow Loop Turner:* Brand name for a one-piece tube turner with a pincer on the end. Slide it through your tube and use the pincer to grip the fabric at the far edge. Then pull the fabric back through to invert the tube.

S E A M S

Seams are the basic components of garments. They serve as the framework. Whether you stitch on a sewing machine, serge, or sew by hand, you should be able to make a straight or a curved seam that lies flat without puckering or pulling. Your seams also should stand up to normal wear. • **Seams can be decorative.** For example, a flat-felled seam not only gives extra strength in heavy fabrics, such as denim, but it also provides an attractive top-stitching accent to the finished garment. Use your serger to create a narrow rolled-edge seam and to add color to garments or to projects such as napkins and tablecloths. • **Stabilizers provide extra body** when you're adding decorative topstitching or embellishing a garment with machine embroidery. Using the right stabilizer for a particular project makes the sewing faster and easier.

Seams hold garments together, so they must be durable and accurate. If your seams are uneven, your finished project may pucker or draw up. If the seam allowance is too wide or too narrow, your garment may not fit.

To make a **seam,** follow these easy directions:

1. Place the right sides of two pieces of fabric together, matching seam edges, the top and bottom of the pieces, and notches or other matching points.

2. Pin the edges, placing pins at right angles to the fabric edge, with the pin heads extending beyond the cut edge (*Diagram A*).

Diagram A: Place pins perpendicular to edge.

3. Make sure the upper thread and the bobbin thread are at the back of the machine, underneath the presser foot. Place the end of the seam under the presser foot, with the edges next to the throatplate marking for the correct seam width. (The most common seam width is ⅝" or 1.5 cm. Check your pattern guide sheet to be sure.)

4. Lower the presser foot. Begin and end each seam by locking the

stitches. Sew two or three stitches with the stitch length set at 0 (or the shortest length available).

5. Change the stitch length to 10 to 12 stitches per inch (the normal setting) for the rest of the seam (*Diagram B*). Remove pins as you come to them.

Diagram B: Keep stitch length even.

Note from Nancy

Keep seams a uniform width by using the seam guide on most sewing machine beds. If your machine doesn't have a seam guide, make your own by measuring carefully and placing a strip of masking tape on your sewing machine so that one edge marks the proper seam width. You can also use Tailor's Triangular Chalk to mark the seam line. This chalk marks a very fine line on fabric and, due to its true chalk base, never leaves a stain.

6. Lock threads at the end of the seam. Turn the balance wheel until the thread take-up lever is at the highest point. (Some machines do this automatically.) Raise the presser foot and gently pull the fabric toward the back of the machine.

7. Cut threads close to the fabric, leaving 2" to 3" (5 cm to 7.5 cm) of thread coming from the needle. Trim the threads at the beginning of the seam, too.

Note from Nancy

Always stop stitching with the needle in the highest position so that the thread take-up lever is also in the highest position. Doing so prevents the thread from pulling out of the needle when you resume stitching.

Test Stitching

Begin by test-stitching a seam on scraps of the fabric you're using for your project. If you're sewing two layers, test with two fabric layers. If you're sewing more layers (as for a collar), test on that number of layers.

Use this test seam to check your machine's tension. The top thread and the bobbin thread of a straight-stitch should connect halfway between the fabric layers. The top thread and the bobbin thread of a zigzag stitch should connect at the corner of each stitch. For either stitch, the seam should lie flat with no puckering, and the threads should not break easily. If your seam doesn't match the proper description, adjust the tension and retest until it does.

Finger Pinning

Try finger pinning when you sew long, straight seams, such as the inner and outer seams of pants. After stitching a seam or two without pins using the finger-pinning method, you'll be convinced that you can sew all long seams in this easy way.

1. To **finger-pin:** place the fabric under the presser foot and lock the stitches, sewing just a few stitches with the stitch length at 0.

2. Match the raw edges at the top end of the seam; pinch the fabric together with your right hand and pull the fabric taut.

3. At the middle of the seam, pinch the raw edges together with your left hand, and transfer them to your right hand without letting go of the end you already pinched (*Photo top right*).

4. Gather the fabric into soft pleats.

    • Match raw edges from the middle of the seam to the bottom (under the presser foot) and pinch them together at 6" to 8" (15 cm to 20 cm) intervals, always transferring the fabric to your right hand. Now you have four to five pleats or "finger pins" of fabric in your right hand.

    • Use your left fingers to hold the fabric layers together by placing your fingers parallel to the seam, as if you were playing the flute.

5. Sew to the first fabric pleat. Release a pleat and continue to sew.

To finger-pin, pinch fabric raw edges together and hold fabric in your right hand.

In a well-made garment, the inside looks as neat as the outside. See page 72 for more on finishing seams.

When you reach the second half of the seam, finger-pin again.

Sew, Press; Sew, Press

Press each seam or construction detail before you join it to another garment section. A good rule is: Sew, press; sew, press. Pressing is different than ironing. When you press, you lift the iron up and down. When you iron, you move the iron back and forth. See page 84 for more information on pressing techniques.

Pressing as you go helps ensure that your seams lie flat and in the proper direction when you join other pieces of the garment or project.

Knit Seams

A conventional zigzag sewing machine has several stitches you can use to seam knits.

For best results, always use stretch or ballpoint needles when you sew knits. If you've worked with knit fabrics before, you may have noticed tiny holes that form along the seam line or topstitching line. The holes are caused by the points of sharp or universal sewing machine needles, which pierce the yarn fibers. Stretch and ballpoint needles have rounded points that slip between the fine knit loops and do not make holes.

To sew a **knit seam:**
1.   Straightstitch along the seam line. Or to provide additional stretch in the seam, use a narrow zigzag stitch (1.5 length, 1.5 width) along the seam line.

2.   Zigzag the seam allowances together, close to the seam line, using a medium-width, medium-length stitch.
3.   Trim the excess seam allowance close to the zigzag stitches.

Another way to add stretch to seams on knit fabric is to stitch using a double needle. The two top threads pass through the twin needles, creating two straight lines of stitching on the top of the fabric, while the bobbin thread zigzags back and forth between the needle threads. Although the double-needle stitch is usually used for hemming and decorative top-stitching, it also builds flexibility into knit seams.

To stitch a **double-needle seam:**
1.   Use one spool of thread on each of the spool pins on top of the machine.

• If your sewing machine has only one spool pin, wind two bobbins and stack the bobbins on the spool pin.
• Follow the threading instructions for your machine, treating both threads as one.
2.   To ensure an accurate ⅝" (1.5 cm) seam, change the needle position so that the left needle lines up with the center of the presser foot. If you can't change the needle position, adjust the ⅝" (1.5 cm) seam guide on the throat plate so that it is ⅝" from the left needle (*Diagram A*).
3.   Stitch the entire garment using a 2.0 mm, 3.0 mm, or 4.0 mm double needle.
4.   Press the seams to one side, hiding the zigzagging. Because of the formation of the stitches, the seams will automatically lap with the double stitching on top.

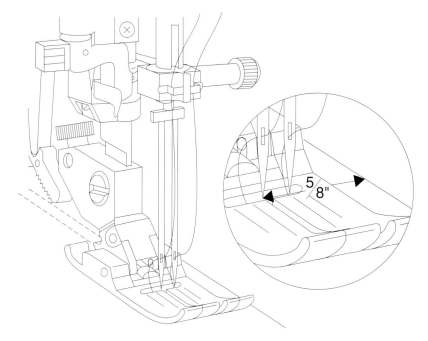

Diagram A: Adjust machine so left needle stitches ⅝" from seam edge.

5. Optional: To stitch a double-needle hem, press under the hem allowance. Then stitch along the hem edge, from the right side, using the double needle.

Topstitching

Most seams are interior details—you won't see them on the outside of a finished garment. Topstitching, however, is decorative stitching that is meant to show on the right side of your finished project.

For a professional-looking garment, be sure that all topstitching lines are an even distance from the edge of the garment. Also, if you're topstitching more than one edge (such as both lapels on a jacket), make sure that all lines of topstitching are the same distance from the edge as each other. (See the first Note from Nancy on page 62 for details on keeping seam widths even.)

When topstitching a garment such as a jacket, you can enhance the look by using two threads in both the needle and the bobbin. If you plan to use only one thread, omit the references to double threads from the instructions below.

To **topstitch** a garment:

1. Insert a topstitching needle in the machine. This needle is available in only a size 90. It has a wider and longer eye that can easily accommodate two strands of sewing machine thread.

2. Wind two threads in the bobbin. You can wind them simultaneously by treating them as one.

3. Adjust the machine settings for topstitching.

• Lengthen the stitch slightly, to about eight stitches per inch.

• Adjust the needle and bobbin tensions.

• Thread the top-thread strands through the machine, treating them as one.

• Thread the bobbin case, treating the two strands as one.

4. Stitch around the edges and seams you want to topstitch, usually about ⅜" from the edge or seam.

To **topstitch knits:**

1. Straightstitch a normal ⅝" (1.5 cm) seam, using a single needle. Press (or finger-press) the seam open.

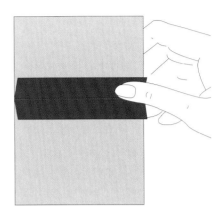

Diagram B: Finger-press by applying pressure with your thumb and index finger.

2. On the right side of the garment, topstitch ⅜" from each side of the seam line, using a medium-length straightstitch (10 to 12 stitches per inch) or a medium-width, medium-length zigzag (*Diagram C*). Use a stretch or ball-point needle, not a topstitching needle.

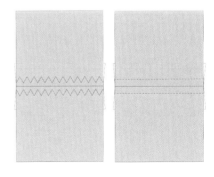

Diagram C: Topstitch knits using a zigzag stitch (left) or a straight-stitch (right).

serger

Serged seams are the norm in ready-to-wear clothing. **Take a look inside purchased T-shirts, sweats, or knit tops. Notice how neat the seams appear.** Sergers trim off excess seam allowances, stitch seams, and overlock edges at the same time.

With a home serger, you can serge garments in minutes, without sacrificing construction quality.

How do you decide whether to serge a seam or to stitch it on a sewing machine? I recommend using serged seams for the following:

• Most knit garments.

• Loose-fitting garments where it isn't important for seams to lie flat.

• When you're sure of the garment's fit, and you will not need to alter seams.

• Where seam allowances don't need to be pressed open.

Basic Serger Stitches

A 3-thread overlock stitch and a 3/4-thread overlock stitch are the two most commonly used serger stitches. You may also want to use a 2-thread overedge stitch, a 2-thread chainstitch, a true 4-thread stitch, or even a 5-thread stitch. Let's look at the difference in these stitches.

• You can produce a **3-thread overlock stitch** on a 3-thread, 4-thread, or 5-thread serger. In this stitch, the threads interlock with the needle thread on the left; the upper and lower looper threads loop together at the fabric's edge (*Diagram A, page 67*). When the looper tensions are balanced, the stitch

looks the same on both sides.

The 3-thread overlock stitch is generally used for seaming or edge-finishing. It is stretchy, making it ideal for knits and versatile for decorative serging. Try heavier threads, ribbons, or yarns in the loopers.

• A **3/4-thread overlock stitch** adds a second line of needle stitching to the right of the primary seam line (*Diagram B, page 67*). The second line of thread runs through both loopers, creating a stitch that is more stable and more durable than the 3-thread overlock stitch.

For specialized serging applications, remove either needle. If you take out the right needle, the left needle makes a wider 3-thread stitch. If you remove the left needle, the right needle makes a narrower 3-thread stitch. You can create intriguing, decorative serging with this stitch.

• The **2-thread overedge stitch**

is formed by thread from one needle and one looper (*Diagram C, page 67*): the needle and upper looper of a 4/2-, 2/3/4-, or 5-thread serger, or the needle and single looper of a 2-thread serger.

The overedge stitch is perfect for finishing edges on lightweight fabrics and for one-step flatlocking, but you must use it in connection with another stitch. Because the upper and lower threads do not lock at the seam line, you cannot use a 2-thread overedge stitch to sew seams.

• The **2-thread chainstitch** is formed by thread from the left needle and from the lower looper thread of a 4/2-thread serger (*Diagram D, page 67*) or a 5-thread serger.

On some sergers, you can disengage the trimming blades so that you can serge this stitch anywhere

Serger Seams

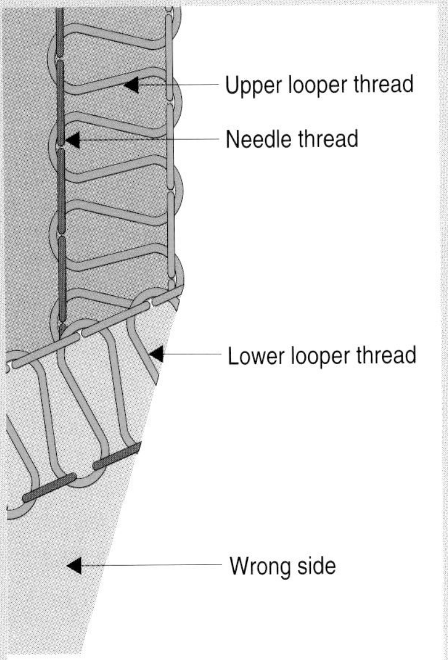

Upper looper thread
Needle thread
Lower looper thread
Wrong side

Diagram A: 3-thread overlock stitch

Upper looper thread
Left needle thread
Right needle thread
Lower looper thread
Wrong side

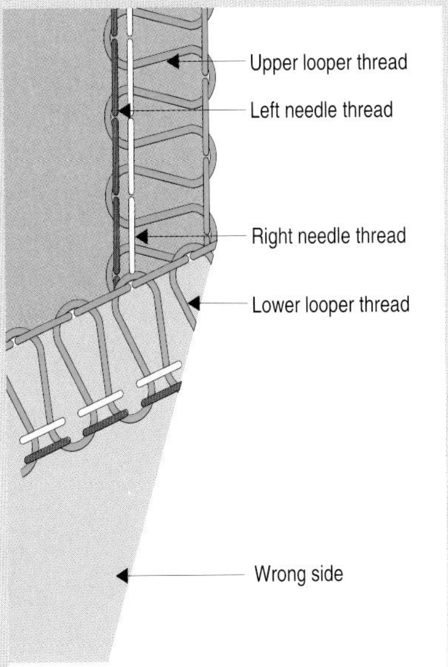

Diagram B: 3/4-thread overlock stitch

Upper looper thread
Needle thread
Needle thread from wrong side
Wrong side

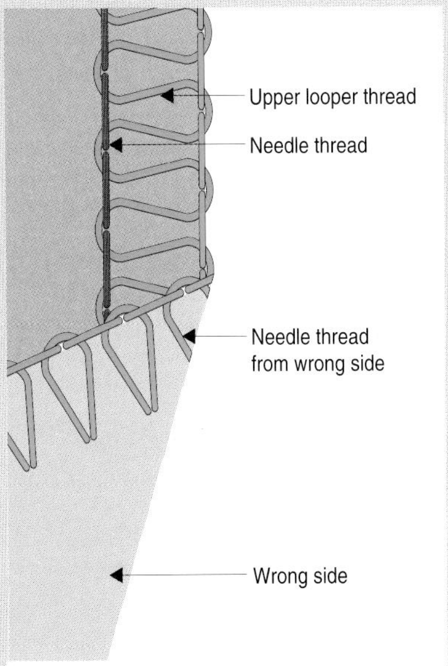

Diagram C: 2-thread overedge stitch

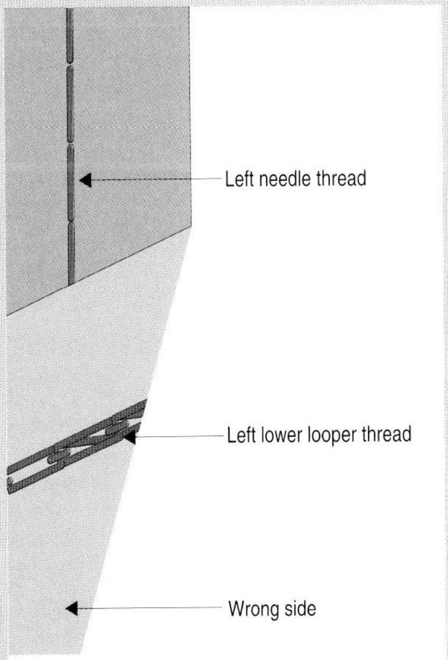

Left needle thread
Left lower looper thread
Wrong side

Diagram D: 2-thread chainstitch

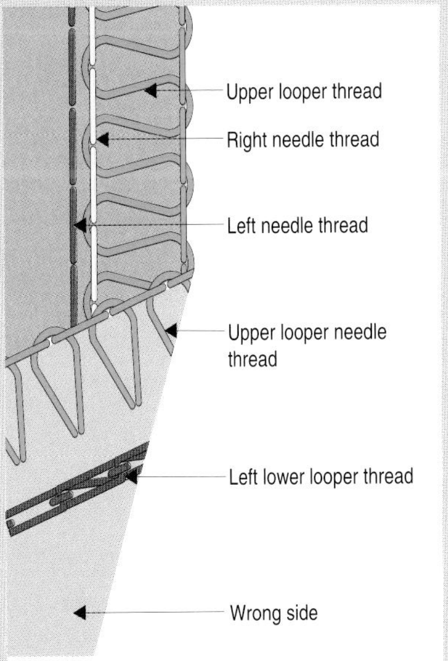

Upper looper thread
Right needle thread
Left needle thread
Upper looper needle thread
Left lower looper thread
Wrong side

Diagram E: True 4-thread overlock stitch

Upper looper thread
Right needle thread
Left needle thread
Right lower looper thread
Right needle thread
Left lower looper thread
Wrong side

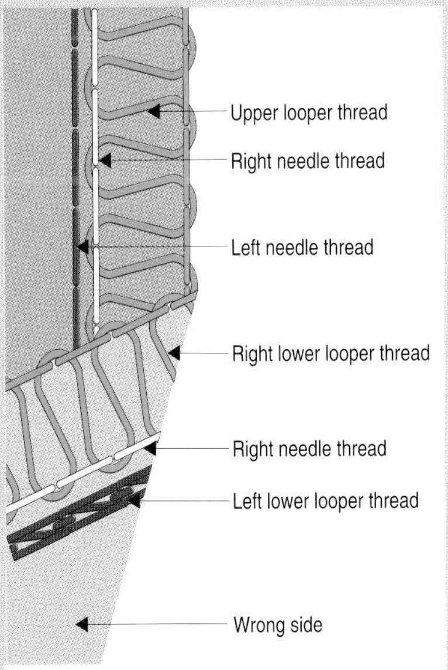

Diagram F: 5-thread overlock stitch

on the fabric, without trimming simultaneously. On other sergers, you can use the chainstitch only along an edge. For decorative top-stitching, especially if you use heavier or decorative thread in the loopers, serge with the right side of the project next to the feed dogs.

• You can serge a **true 4-thread overlock stitch** only on a machine that has 4/2-thread capability, such as a 4/2-thread serger and most 5-thread sergers. This stitch combines a 2-thread chainstitch with a 2-thread overedge stitch (*Diagram E, page 67*). It is best suited for use on woven fabrics or for stabilizing stretchy fabrics.

• The **5-thread overlock stitch** is the strongest of all serger seams. The machine uses five threads at one time—two threads to form a double chainstitch and three threads to overlock the edges (*Diagram F, page 67*).

Safe Pinning

For garments you plan to serge, place pins parallel to the seam and 1" from the cut edges (*Diagram G*). Don't pin at right angles to the seam (as you do when stitching on a conventional machine). If you do, the serger knives might cut into a pin you forget to remove, dulling or damaging the blades.

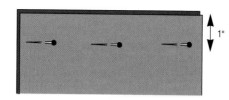

Diagram G: Place pins parallel to fabric edges for serging.

Note from Nancy

I like to use flower head pins when serging. The flower heads lie flat against the fabric, yet they're easy to grasp and easy to locate when you're serging a seam. Plus, because the pins are extra long (2"), you need fewer pins for each seam.

Accurate Seam Allowances

You can set the width of a serged seam from ⅛" to ⅜" (3 mm to 10 mm)—perfect for patterns with ¼" seam allowances. But if your pattern has allowed for ⅝" (1.5 cm) seams, align the cut edges of the garment pieces with the seam-width guide printed on the serger's looper cover.

If your serger does not have these markings, determine a point ⅝" (1.5 cm) from the needle, so that the needle will stitch on the pattern seam line. Mark this position with a piece of tape.

Ravel-Proofing Seam Ends

You should secure serged seams at the beginning and the end as you do with seams stitched on a sewing machine. But because a serger does not backstitch, you'll need to try one of these alternative methods to secure the thread ends:

• Apply a drop of seam sealant on the end of the seam. Allow it to dry and then clip the thread tail. The common seam sealants (Fray Check and No-Fray) are made of a waterproof silicone solution that doesn't wash out. A drop is all you need at the end of a serged seam.

• Use a darning needle or a large-eyed needle to bury the thread tail under the looper threads.

Serger Seams for Knits

Because a serger finishes a seam's raw edge as it stitches, it's great for seaming stretchy knits. To serge seams on knit fabrics, use a 3- or 3/4-thread overlock stitch adjusted for balanced tension. Unless color matching is critical, use all-purpose serger thread in the needle and in both loopers.

I love to stitch by machine or on my serger, and I have found that I can do almost all my sewing this way. However, there are times when you may need to handstitch something. Also, many people enjoy the pleasure and portability of hand sewing.

Getting Ready

Choose the right type of needle (see page 50). You should use a needle that makes as small a hole as possible. However, it should be heavy enough to go through the type of fabric and number of layers you'll be sewing without bending or breaking.

For most handstitching, use a single strand of thread. To reduce thread tangling, thread a needle using the end of the thread that came off the spool. Trim the end of the thread on the diagonal so that it's freshly cut and not frayed.

If you have trouble threading a needle, or if the needle has a small eye, try using a needle threader. This helpful tool has a wire loop that you place through the needle's eye. Once the needle threader is in place, insert the end of your thread through the wire loop, and pull the threader back through the needle's eye.

A quilter's knot is a good beginning knot for most handsewing tasks. Knot the end of the thread that you cut last, rather than the end you threaded through the needle. To tie a **quilter's knot,** follow these instructions:

1. Hold the threaded needle between your thumb and forefinger about halfway down the needle shaft. Pick up the long end of the

thread (the thread tail) with your other hand and place it on top of the needle, allowing the end to extend about ½" (1.3 cm) beyond the needle (*Diagram A*).

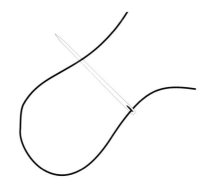

Diagram A: Place thread tail on top of needle.

2. Pinch the thread tail between the thumb and forefinger, pressing it against the needle.
3. With your other hand, wrap the section of the thread between the needle and the eye around the needle three times (*Diagram B*). The number of wraps determines how big the knot is; wrap more times for a larger knot. Pinch the wraps between your thumb and finger.
4. While pinching the wraps and

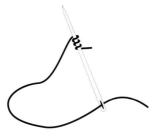

Diagram B: Wrap thread tail around needle shaft.

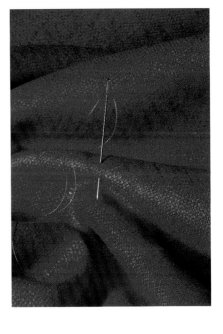

the needle with one hand, let go of the long thread with the other hand. Grasp the needle near the point and pull the needle through the wraps. While pulling the needle, continue to pinch the wraps gently with your fingers until you have pulled all the thread through the wraps, forming a firm knot (*Diagram C*). If you failed to form a knot, you may have wrapped the short end of the thread rather than the long end.

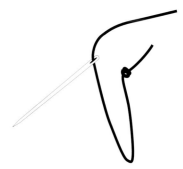

Diagram C: Pull needle through wraps to form a quilter's knot.

5. Clip the thread tail near the knot.

Once you've threaded your needle and knotted your thread, you may also want to run the thread through beeswax to give it more strength and to reduce tangling further. Beeswax is available in a holder suitable for coating thread and is sold in most fabric stores and through mail-order notions catalogs.

Hand-Sewing Stitches

Considering the variety of embroidery stitches, there are hundreds of decorative handstitches. However, a few basic stitches are especially useful to garment sewers.

• A **backstitch** is a durable handstitch, useful for repairing seams, sewing garments when a machine isn't available, or stitching zippers by hand. To make a backstitch, bring the needle up on the seam line. Take a stitch backward and bring the needle up an equal distance ahead of the first hole made by the needle. Repeat, taking the needle back to the end of the previous stitch (*Diagram A*).

You can finish a project completely by machine, but many of us still prefer to sew on buttons and stitch other parts by hand.

• A **basting stitch** or **running stitch** is useful for temporarily sewing pieces together. Weave the tip of the needle through the fabric, grouping three to five stitches on the needle, depending on your stitch length (*Diagram B*). Pull the needle and thread through the fabric. The stitches should look the same on the front and the back. In addition to using the running stitch to baste, you can use it to mark pattern pieces or to help ease fullness in sleeves and other garment sections.

• Use the **blindhem stitch** to sew a hem quickly and almost invisibly. Finish the hem edge by zigzagging, serging, or turning under the raw edge of the hem. Then fold back the garment edge so that about 1/4" (6 mm) of the hem edge shows (*Diagram C, page 71*). Take a tiny stitch in the hem, and then take a tiny stitch in the garment about 1/4" (6 mm) ahead of the first stitch (*Diagram D, page 71*), picking up only one or two threads in the fabric. Next take a stitch in the hem edge about 1/4" (6 mm) ahead of the last stitch. Repeat, alternating stitches between the hem edge and the

Diagram A: Backstitch

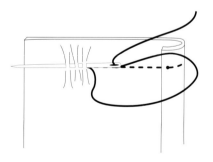

Diagram B: Basting/running stitch

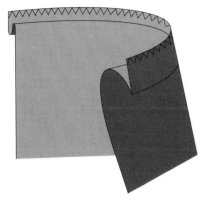

Diagram C: For a blindhem stitch, fold back garment edge.

Diagram D: Take a stitch in hem and then one in garment.

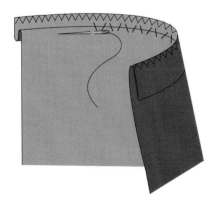

Diagram E: Repeat blindhem stitches across hem.

garment (*Diagram E*). Don't pull the stitches too tight or the hem will pucker.

• A **whipstitch** (also called an **overcasting stitch**) is used for joining pieces. This stitch is commonly used to join crocheted or hand-knitted garment pieces. To make a whipstitch, fold under the seam allowances of each piece to be whipstitched. With right sides of folded fabric edges together, insert the needle through both folds, barely catching the edges. Insert your needle close to the previous stitch through both folds, and gently pull the thread through to hold pieces together (*Diagram F*). Don't pull tight or the stitches will distort the fabrics.

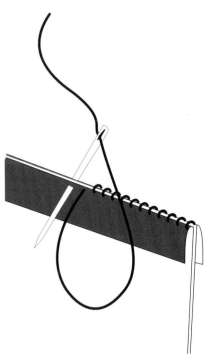

Diagram F: Whipstitch/overcasting stitch

"Reverse sewing" (taking out seams) is a hand-sewing project. To take out serged seams, use a sharp serger seam remover like the one pictured. For sewn seams, use a sharp seam ripper or a pair of sharp scissors with narrow points. Clip a single stitch every inch or so along the seam and carefully pick out remaining thread.

finishing

After stitching a seam, add a finish to each seam edge to prevent fraying and to give the seams a neater look. To avoid bulk and make the seam flatter and neater, you should stitch most seam finishes on a single layer of fabric.

Choose one of the following **seam finishes:**

1. Zigzag each seam edge. Zigzagging works best on medium-weight to heavyweight fabrics. If zigzagging draws in the seam edge and makes it pucker, choose another seam finish.

• Use a medium-width zigzag and a medium to short stitch length.

• Stitch the zig in the fabric and the zag close to or off the cut edge.

Use Seams Great to encase raw edges and to give the inside of your projects a professional look.

> ## Note from Nancy
>
> *If fabric edges almost always curl and pucker when you zigzag, try replacing the regular presser foot with an overcast-guide foot. (See page 151 for a diagram of this foot.) The overcast-guide foot holds fabric flat while the zigzag goes over the fabric edge. You can usually buy this foot as a separate accessory.*

2. Clean-finish by folding under each seam edge before edgestitching (see option 6). Fold under 1/8" (3 mm) for most fabrics, and 1/4" (6 mm) if the fabric ravels easily.

3. Serge each seam edge using a 3-thread or 3/4-thread overlock stitch.

4. Pink the edges by cutting along each seam edge using pinking shears.

5. Enclose the raw edges in Seams Great, a 5/8"-wide nylon fabric. Place the raw edge of the fabric within the curl of the Seams Great, and straightstitch or zigzag it in place (*photo above*).

6. If your machine doesn't have a zigzag stitch, edgestitch close to each seam edge. Set the machine to a straightstitch. Guide the right edge of the presser foot along the cut edge of the fabric. Stitching should be about 1/4" (6 mm) from the cut edge.

Reducing Seam Bulk

Some seams require you to do more than press them before you're done. In heavyweight or bulky fabrics, you usually need to reduce the seam's bulk. For curved seams, such as princess seams and some neckline seams, you may need to clip the seam allowance to make the seam lie flat.

To reduce bulk in a seam, trim the finished seam allowance to about half its original width. That means that, if you sewed a 5/8" (1.5 cm) seam allowance, you should trim the finished seam allowance to about 3/8".

If the seam still doesn't lie flat, grade it. To do this, leave the seam allowance that is closest to the garment at its new width, but trim the other seam allowance another 1/4" (6 mm) or so. This eliminates the bulky ridge that can show on the outside when you press the garment over the seam allowance.

When you sew curved seams, seam allowances with inward curves have too much fabric, which bunches up when you press. Seam allowances with outward curves have too little fabric, which causes the garment fabric to pull when you press.

To solve the problem of inward curves (too much fabric), clip or nip the seam allowances by cutting slits in the seam allowance at regular intervals (*Diagram*). Be careful not to cut into the seam itself. These clips remove the extra fabric in the seam allowance, letting it lie flat.

For outward curves (too little fabric), notch the seam allowance. That means cut small V shapes out of the seam allowance at regular intervals, being careful not to cut into the seam line. The notches allow the seam allowance fabric to

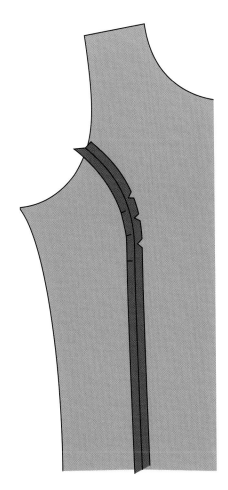

Diagram: Clip on inward curves (left) and notch on outward curves (right).

spread and the seam to press flat. Restitch the seam after clipping or notching.

If you have an outward curve sewn to an inward curve (such as a princess seam), notch the outward curve of the seam allowance and clip the inward curve. Offset the two types of seam allowance treatments. For example, if you put a notch directly opposite a clip, you will weaken the seam.

For facings and other seam allowances, you may need to understitch in order to get the seam allowance to lie flat. Many patterns include understitching in their instructions for facings and similar seams. To understitch a facing, simply stitch through the facing and the seam allowance, very close to the connecting seam.

Besides basic straightstitch and zigzag seams, there are many special seams you can use that are suited to specific fabrics or garment styles. These include curved princess seams that add shape to a garment, French seams that enclose raw edges on sheer fabrics, and special exposed seams for Ultrasuede.

Princess Seams

A princess seam is a combination of a seam and a dart, providing both shape and style in a garment. The two sections joined in a princess seam are of different lengths, which sometimes makes it challenging to stitch the two areas together.

Use your sewing machine's feed dogs to help you join these seam edges. The process is so simple— yet it makes such a difference in the garment's appearance.

To make a **princess seam:**
1. Examine the pattern pieces for a princess seam to help you visualize

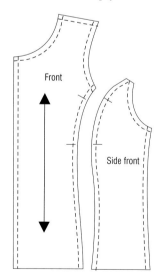

Diagram A: Princess seam

how the seam joins (*Diagram A*).
- The front has a short outward curve.
- The side front has a long inward curve where the dart would otherwise be incorporated. You must ease this excess fabric into the smaller front curve.
2. Examine how your sewing machine handles fabric as it moves through the machine.
- The feed dogs bite the fabric and ease it through the machine.
- To join fabric pieces of different lengths, stitch with the longer section facing the feed dogs to help ease it into the shorter section.
3. Stitch the seam.
- Disengage the walking foot or dual feed if your machine has those features. Both features counteract the easing action of the feed dogs. You want to use that easing action.
- Use ease stitching rather than directional stitching, and always stitch with the longer layer toward the feed dogs. On one seam, this means stitching from the bottom toward the top. On the other, it means stitching from the top toward the bottom.

- When stitching the curved area, insert your left hand between the fabric layers, and use your right fingertips to align the cut areas.
4. Press the seam.
- First, press the seam flat, with the longer layer facing the ironing board. In the curved area, use the tip of the iron to press the seam so that you don't flatten the eased fabric.
- Press the seam open over a seam roll, or use a Seam Stick. The wooden Seam Stick is a pressing tool with a flat side and a rounded side that provides a crisp pressed edge without seam imprints.

5. Clip and notch seam allowances where needed after pressing.
- Notch to release tension on the shorter front section.
- Clip so fullness can overlap on the longer side front.

French Seams

For very sheer fabrics or fabrics that ravel easily, French seams enclose the seam allowances, giving a neat finish that practically eliminates ravelling. French seams are a perfect choice for joining fabrics such as batiste, chiffon, and voile. With two rows of straightstitching and a little pressing, you encase the raw edges of the fabric attractively and neatly.

To stitch a **French seam:**

1.   With wrong sides together and raw edges aligned, straightstitch ³⁄₈" from the cut edges.

2.   Using a rotary cutter and cutting mat, trim the seam allowance to just slightly less than ¹⁄₄" or 6 mm (*Diagram B*).

Diagram B: Trim seam allowances to slightly less than ¼".

3.   Press the joined edges flat and then press the seam open. This makes it easier to fold the seam allowance along the first stitching line in preparation for the second row of machine stitching.

4.   Refold the seam allowance with the right sides of the fabric together, positioning the first stitch-ing line at the fold. To complete the French seam, stitch ¹⁄₄" (6 mm) from the fold, encasing the cut edges (*Diagram C*).

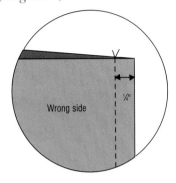

Diagram C: Stitch second row of stitching ¼" from fold.

Note from Nancy

To save time, I often reverse the width of the seam allowances, stitching the ¼" seam first, then the ⅜" seam. This method produces a slightly wider seam, but it reduces the trimming step. For extremely sheer fabric, the narrower width is best.

Seams for Ultrasuede

Synthetic suede, such as Ultrasuede, is a nonwoven, napped fabric that's easy to work with. Because it does not ravel, you don't have to sew traditional seams. For a more sporty look, you can sew a lapped seam and leave the exposed edges unfinished.

Try this **exposed overlapped seam** to speed sewing:

1.   Prepare the pieces to be stitched.

• Use chalk or a fabric marking pencil to mark a ¹⁄₂" (1.3 cm) seam allowance along one edge of one piece.

• Lap the edge of the unmarked piece over the marked line, extending its edge slightly beyond the marking (*Diagram D*). The finished over-lapped seam will be ⁵⁄₈" (1.5 cm).

Diagram D: Overlap edges to make a seam on Ultrasuede.

• Use a fabric glue stick or a liquid adhesive, such as Insta-Pin, to hold the two layers together temporarily. You could pin these layers together, but because Ultrasuede is quite dense, pinning can be difficult. Also, bubbles sometimes form in pinned areas. Using an adhesive gives a smoother, neater seam and simplifies stitching.

2.   Join the seam with two rows of topstitching.

• Use a double needle as a fast way of stitching overlapped seams. A double needle produces two parallel rows of stitching on top of the fabric; you can use it on any zigzag sewing machine that threads from front to back. Use a 4.0/100 or 3.0/90 double needle to edgestitch the seam. (See page 64 for more information on stitching with double needles.)

• Mark a line or locate a position on your machine presser foot so that the first line of stitching is about ⅛" (3 mm) from the cut edge. Stitch each seam at the same position so that all seams look uniform.

• As an alternative to double-needle stitching, stitch two parallel rows of straightstitching along the "pinned" seam, using a size 75 Microtex needle. Because Ultrasuede is a very dense fabric, it can be hard to stitch through using a universal-point needle. A Microtex needle has a special point that more easily pierces the fabric and helps prevent skipped stitches.

•• Stitch the first row ⅛" (3 mm) from the edge and the second ¼" (6 mm) from the first row.

•• Use the edge of the presser foot to help keep the stitching straight. The toes on many presser feet are ¼" (6 mm) wide, so positioning the edge of the foot along the first row of stitching produces two parallel rows of stitching ¼" (6 mm) apart.

In addition to overlapped seams, you can make two other special

The shoulders of this Ultrasuede vest have overlapped seams. The rest of the garment has exposed-edge seams, which have been embellished using narrow ribbon and a running stitch.

types of seams on Ultrasuede: "kissed" seams and exposed-edge seams. I recommend using kissed seams for facings and other inside details to eliminate the bulk of the seam allowances.

To make a **kissed seam:**

1. Use a size 75 stretch needle to help prevent skipped stitches.

2. Cut a 1"-wide (2.5 cm-wide) strip of fusible interfacing.

3. Trim off the seam allowances of the facing.

4. Position the wrong sides of the pieces to be joined over the interfacing, butting the cut edges where pieces would otherwise be seamed. Meet the fusible side of the interfacing to the wrong side of the fabric.

5. Stitch along each butted suede edge using a serpentine stitch, a mul-

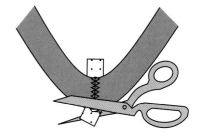

Diagram: Trim excess interfacing to finish a kissed Ultrasuede seam.

tiple zigzag stitch, or a straightstitch. Backstitch to secure threads at each end of the seam.

6. Trim excess interfacing at the top and bottom of the stitched pieces (*Diagram*).

7. Fuse interfacing to Ultrasuede, covering the fabric with a press cloth and pressing from the wrong side.

An **exposed-edge seam** is especially useful for areas where you're attaching facings to an Ultrasuede garment.

1. Prepare the seam.

• Before cutting out the garment, cut off all seam allowances from the main pattern pieces. If you want to use the pattern later for other fabrics, either fold back the seam allowances or make duplicate pattern pieces in waxed paper.

• Keep the ⅝" (1.5 cm) seam allowance on the facing. Mark the ⅝" (1.5 cm) seam line on the wrong side of the facing (*Diagram A*).

2. With wrong sides together, overlap the garment cut edge to the seam line marked on the facing edge (*Diagram B*). Pin or glue edges together.

3. Topstitch the garment and facing together, positioning one row of stitching ⅛" (3 mm) from the garment edge and the other ¼" (6 mm) from the first row of stitches. Use a double needle to stitch both rows at the same time.

4. Trim the facing seam allowance, guiding the shears next to the cut edge of the garment (*Diagram C*). Trimming after topstitching allows you to get a sharp, crisp line at the outer edge.

Exposed-Edge Seam for Ultrasuede

Diagram A: Mark seam line on wrong side of facing.

Diagram B: Overlap garment and facing, wrong sides together.

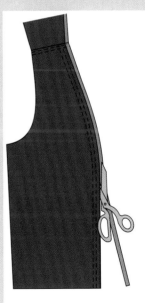

Diagram C: Topstitch; then trim exposed-edge seam.

decorative SERGED SEAMS

Serged seams provide a neat, clean finish for the inside edges of knit garments and other items. But you can also use your serger to create decorative finishes.

Try using decorative threads in the looper(s) and then purposely exposing the seam. Take a few extra minutes to test a decorative serging technique on scraps of your fabric.

To make a **decorative serged seam:**

1. Serge, with wrong sides together, along the ⅝" (1.5 cm) seam line. The serger's blades trim the excess seam allowance width while serging.

2. Select a medium-to-wide stitch width and a short stitch length, and put decorative thread in the upper looper. Try using woolly nylon (texturized nylon thread) or Decor 6 (rayon decorative thread) in the upper looper. (For more decorative thread, see page 155.)

• Serge the seam so that the decorative serging shows.

• Finger-press the seam to one side.

• Edgestitch the seam to the fabric using a conventional sewing machine.

Decorative Serged Hems

If you use a decorative stitch to serge the seams, try decoratively serging the hem to unify the garment's design elements.

To sew a **decorative serged hem:**

1. Select a medium-to-wide stitch width and a short stitch length, and put decorative thread in the upper looper. With the wrong side of the garment facing up, serge along the edge of the hem. (You serge only a single layer of fabric.) To produce a more uniform stitch, allow the serger blades to trim the edge of the hem slightly.

2. Press the hem to the right side, exposing the decorative serging. With a conventional sewing machine, edgestitch along the serged needle line to complete the hem.

Narrow Rolled-Edge Seams

Before the introduction of home-use sergers, only factory workrooms could produce the narrow rolled edges seen on napkins, scarves, and tablecloths. Now, with only a few adjustments, you, too, can serge this lovely, lightweight stitch.

To create a **narrow rolled-edge seam,** convert a 3-thread overlock or a 2-thread overedge stitch to a rolled-edge stitch. Tension adjustments are crucial. General adjustment guidelines for converting to a narrow rolled edge are listed below; check your owner's manual for the exact settings for your serger.

1. Replace the standard foot with the rolled-edge foot, which has a narrower stitch finger than the standard foot (*Diagram A*). On some sergers, the stitch finger is on a separate throat plate instead of on the presser foot; if your serger is designed this way, change the throat plate. Other sergers require changing both the foot and the throat plate. A few sergers may require dropping part of the stitch finger (narrowing the width), rather than changing either the foot or the throat plate.

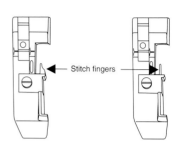

Diagram A: A standard foot (left) has a wider stitch finger than a rolled-edge foot (right).

2. Narrow the stitch width as much as possible, and shorten the setting on the stitch-length dials. Begin with a setting of 2 mm for the stitch length and adjust as necessary.

3. If you are using a 3/4-thread serger, remove the left needle.

4. Tighten the lower-looper tension considerably.

5. Test the stitch and adjust the tensions as necessary to achieve the desired look. With the upper-looper tension loosened and the lower-looper tension tightened, the thread from the upper looper should roll over the edge (*Diagram B*).

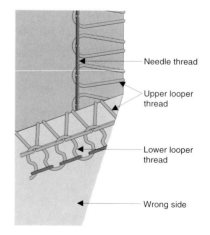

Needle thread
Upper looper thread
Lower looper thread
Wrong side

Diagram B: Rolled-edge seam

6. Use the following guidelines for rolled-edge troubleshooting.

• If you get "pokies"—whiskers of fabric poking through the rolled edge, especially on the crosswise grain (*Diagram C*)—shorten the stitch length. If that doesn't solve the problem, widen the stitch bite (the distance between the blade and the needle). For specific instructions, see your owner's manual or ask your dealer. Or use a multifilament thread (woolly nylon) that spreads over the edge (almost a must!).

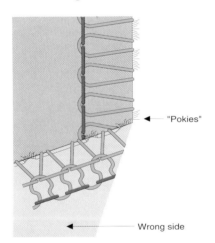

Diagram C: "Pokies" may stick out of rolled edges.

• If the edge doesn't roll to the underside (*Diagram D*), tighten the lower-looper tension. Or use texturized or monofilament nylon thread in the lower looper.

Note from Nancy

Don't rule out using a narrow unrolled edge. For this easy stitch, use the narrow stitch, but keep the tension balanced. I use it when a fabric is particularly resistant to rolling or if I want to expose a lower looper thread that's decorative.

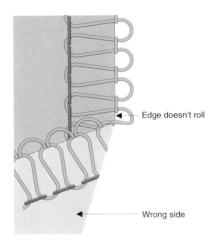

Diagram D: Sometimes the edge doesn't roll.

• If the edge puckers, loosen the needle tension. If the looper tension adjustments are straining the needle line, tighten the needle tension.

• If the stitches pull off the fabric (*Diagram E*), lengthen the stitch. You'll encounter this problem more on lightweight fabrics because the short stitching is too dense for these types of fabric. If lengthening the stitch doesn't work, widen the stitch bite. (See your owner's manual.) Or change the direction in which you're serging. (The lengthwise grain and the bias are less likely to ravel than the crosswise grain.)

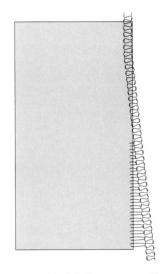

Diagram E: Stitches may pull off the fabric.

Decorative Flatlocking

Flatlocking is a serging technique that uses two or three threads with very loose thread tension on the wrong side of the garment. You serge two layers of fabric together, and then gently pull until the fabric is flat. The result is a versatile stitch you can use for both decorative seaming and topstitching (see *Diagram A* on page 80).

Just about any serger can flatlock—all you need is 3-thread or 2-thread stitch capability. Check your owner's manual or workbook for specific recommendations. General guidelines for 3-thread flatlocking are on the next page.

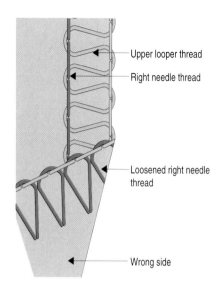

Upper looper thread

Right needle thread

Loosened right needle thread

Wrong side

Diagram A: Flatlocking

To create the **flatlock stitch:**

1.   If seaming, pretrim excess seam allowances. Although it's best to test the width of the flatlock seam on scraps, you can estimate that the seam will be about ¼" (5 mm to 6 mm).

2.   If topstitching with flatlocking (on a fold), fold the fabric with wrong sides together along the line you want to embellish.

3.   Use the standard presser foot and stitch finger.

4.   Loosen the needle tension to 0 or as much as possible.

5.   Tighten the lower looper by four to five settings.

6.   Leave the upper looper at the normal tension setting.

7.   Guide the fabric away from the serger blade.

8.   Use only the left needle of a 3/4-thread or 5-thread serger; this gives the widest flatlock stitch.

9.   Test the stitch on a scrap of fabric. For the flattest flatlocking, guide the fabric to the left of the blade, so that the stitches hang over the edge slightly (*Diagram B*). Doing this allows space for the fabric under the stitch and prevents the problem of accidentally cutting the fabric if you're flatlocking a fold.

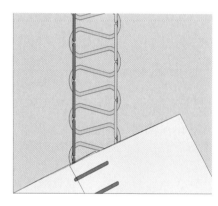

Diagram B: Guide fabric so that stitches hang over edge.

Note from Nancy

To serge the best flatlock stitch, tighten the lower looper thread to form a straight line. In addition to adjusting the tension dials, you can tighten the lower looper thread by using texturized woolly nylon thread. This thread stretches as it passes through the guides, increasing the tightening action. Another alternative is to use finger tensioning.

10.   Grasp the fabric on both sides of the stitches and gently pull to flatten (*Diagram C*).

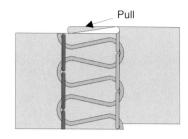

Pull

Diagram C: Pull gently from both sides until fabric lies flat.

11.   Follow the guidelines below to troubleshoot any problems you have with flatlocking.

•   If the stitching doesn't pull completely flat, loosen the needle tension.

•   If you've loosened it as much as possible, then remove the needle thread from the tension disk or dial. If your serger has drop-in tension dials, cover the needle-tension slot with a piece of transparent tape. Or if your machine has knob-type dials, don't engage the thread in the dial. When flatlocking, allow the stitches to hang slightly over the edge.

Note from Nancy

Flatlocking usually requires no tension adjustment at all, if you have a serger with 2-thread overedge capability, such as a 2/3/4-thread, some 5-thread, and some late-model 2-thread machines. Serge the fold or edge, pull it flat, and voilà!—it's flatlocked. When you use heavier fabrics or threads, you may need to loosen both the needle and the looper tensions.

CHOOSING stabilizers

When you're sewing on slippery fabrics, such as satin, or creating decorative stitches, using a stabilizer helps to support the fabric and make stitching easier.

Stabilizers add body to fabric and prevent puckering, pulling, or tearing of stitches on delicate and stretchy fabrics. Back your fabric with stabilizer before stitching, and then tear, press, or wash the stabilizer away when you finish your sewing or embellishing.

When sewing slippery or delicate fabrics, use a stabilizer to ease the process. To keep your sewing machine from drawing lightweight fabrics, such as batiste, organdy, and chiffon, under the throat plate, begin sewing a seam on a piece of tear-away stabilizer. Then place the fabric on top of the stabilizer and continue stitching to complete the seam.

Sometimes when you stitch on soft, lightweight fabrics, such as chiffon and georgette, the seams tend to pucker or stretch no matter how you adjust the tension. If that happens, try sandwiching the fabric between two layers of tissue paper. Stitch the seam and then carefully tear away the tissue paper, taking care not to damage or distort the stitching.

To determine which type of stabilizer to use for a particular project, consider the weight of the fabric and the type of stitching. Here are some suggestions to guide your selection:

• **Iron-on stabilizer** can be pressed to the back of fabric using a lukewarm iron. The waxy backing temporarily bonds the paper to the fabric. After you finish stitching, you can peel the paper away.

Because this type of stabilizer temporarily bonds to fabric, it stabilizes knits by keeping them from stretching. Iron-on stabilizer is inexpensive and is effective for stabilizing large areas, but it works better with dense satin stitches than with more delicate stitching. You can also use **freezer paper** from your grocery store as an iron-on stabilizer.

• **Liquid stabilizer** gives body to fabric and then washes away after stitching. Apply it straight from the bottle, let it dry, and then stitch.

• **Nonwoven tear-away stabilizer** looks and feels much like a heavy, nonwoven interfacing. It is perhaps the most versatile stabilizer and works well with a wide variety of light and heavyweight fabrics. Tear-away stabilizer is best suited for decorative stitches that are close together, such as dense satin stitching. Always test the stabilizer on a fabric scrap before working on the project to be sure you don't damage the stitching when you tear away the stabilizer.

• **Water-soluble stabilizer** completely dissolves in water. After it's removed, you can easily eliminate any residue by spritzing the project with water. Water-soluble stabilizer is more delicate than other stabilizers, making it especially suited for delicate, open decorative stitches and for stretch stitches. Store water-soluble stabilizer in a closed plastic bag to prevent it from becoming crisp or brittle.

See page 146 for a chart of different kinds of stabilizers.

Stabilizers come in many varieties, including the water-soluble type used here. Once the stitching is done, you simply spritz the project with water to get rid of the stabilizer.

TECHNIQUES

The step-by-step instructions on your pattern guide sheet tell you what to do to make a garment, but the guide sheet doesn't always tell you how to complete each step. And it doesn't offer any help when you make a mistake. • **Sometimes knowing a special way to complete a technique can save you time,** give you more professional-looking results, or both. Some of these techniques, such as pressing and putting in a dart, are basic. Others, such as gathering with Clear Elastic and inserting a sleeve lining while hemming the sleeve, save you time. Other techniques, such as stitching a double welt pocket and making your own shoulder pads, give your garments a couture look. • **Use your serger to streamline your sewing.** If you're new to serging—or if you've serged only very basic seams—you'll find new ways to let a serger simplify your sewing.

The difference between a garment that looks professionally stitched and one that looks homemade is often the way in which it's pressed. Never delay pressing until the garment is completed—always press every step of the way. Press each seam or construction detail before you cross it with another seam or construction detail.

Pressing Straight Seams

Here's a quick method for pressing **straight seams:**

1.   Press the seam flat. This sets the stitching and makes it easier to press the seam open.

2.   Place the seam over a seam roll and press it open (*Diagram A*). Using a seam roll prevents the imprint of seam edges from showing on the right side of the fabric.

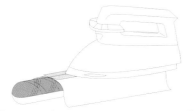

Diagram A: Press seam over seam roll.

This two-step technique works well on virtually all straight seams, but some fabrics require special treatment.

Acrylic knits: Less is best when pressing these fabrics. Sweater knits can be difficult to press. To prevent stretching, steam the seam, and then finger-press. Avoid touching the iron to the fabric's surface. This can sometimes leave a shine on the knit that is hard to remove.

Napped fabrics: When pressing napped fabrics, such as corduroy, velvet, and velveteen, be careful not to flatten the nap. Here's how:

Cover the ironing surface with a needleboard, such as Velvaboard, or a piece of the napped fabric to prevent crushing the pile. Velvaboard is a heat-resistant, bristled nylon pile mat with a latex coating and Teflon® backing that captures steam and reflects it back up into the fabric (*Photo A*).

Photo A: Use a Velvaboard to press napped fabrics.

Place the right side of the garment over the right side of the Velvaboard, and steam the area. Be sure to hold the iron above the fabric rather than resting it on the garment. Finger-press the seam. This helps eliminate puckers and prevents flattening the nap.

Ribbed knits: Finger-press ribbed knits rather than using an iron. For pointed edges on collars or tabs, insert a Bamboo Pointer & Creaser and then finger-press.

Tapestry or textured fabrics: Seam edges often show on the right side of textured fabrics, even when

you press them over a seam roll. To prevent this, insert strips of adding machine tape or other paper between the seam allowance and the garment before you press it (*Diagram B*).

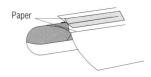

Diagram B: Put paper between seam allowance and garment when pressing.

Wool: The key to pressing wool is using the right press cloth. Use a moisture-holding cloth, such as the Steam 'n Shape Press Cloth. Press the seam flat, cover it with a press cloth, and press the seam open over a seam roll.

When pressing the right side of a wool garment, always use a press cloth between the iron and the fabric.

Pressing Curved Seams

You get the best results if you press curved seams over similar curves. A Tailor Board has a variety of shapes and angles suited for pressing most curves (*Photo B*). Match the shape to be pressed to the same shape on the Tailor Board. Press open curved seams in collars, cuffs, and lapels before turning them right side out to get crisper, flatter edges.

To press a **curved seam,** use this technique:

1.   Press the curve flat.

2.   Press the curve open over the pressing board.

•   Press on the board's wooden

Photo B: A Tailor Board has shapes to help you press.

surface for details requiring sharp points and crisp edges.

• Add a pad to the board when pressing details that should be shaped into the garment.

3. Trim curved seams after you press them open.

Pressing Serged Seams

Because you stitch and finish serged seams in one operation, you must use slightly different pressing techniques. To press a **serged seam:**

1. Press the seam flat, just as you do for sewn seams.

2. Next, position the seam over a seam roll, and press the seam to one side (*Diagram C*).

3. With heavier fabrics, put strips of adding machine tape or other paper under the seam to prevent an imprint from showing on the right side.

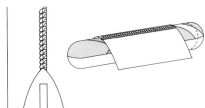

Diagram C: Press serged seams flat; then press to one side over seam roll.

4. After pressing, check the right side of the garment to be sure you didn't press a fold at the seam line. You may need to press again from the right side, using a press cloth.

Setting Pants Creases

Creating perfect pants creases is easier than you think! Follow the custom technique or the quick technique for super-sharp creases.

Custom Technique

1. Set the front crease first.

• Meet the cut edges of the pants front at the hem and the crotch (*Diagram D*).

• Cover the fold with a press cloth to avoid damaging the fabric's surface or creating a shine.

• Steam a small section.

• Place a clapper on the steamed area, and press down firmly until the area is cool and dry (*Photo C*). This action forces out moisture and produces a sharp crease. Repeat until you've pressed the entire crease.

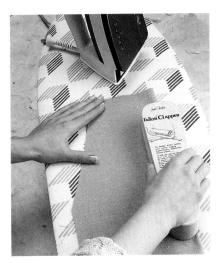

Photo C: Use clapper to set pants creases.

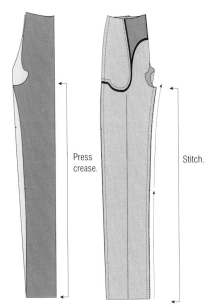

Diagram D: Set front crease (left). Sew front and back together at inseam and outer seam (right).

2. After setting the front crease, sew front and back pants pieces together at the inseam and outer seam (*Diagram D*).

3. Set the back crease.

• Use the front crease to determine the back crease. Match the inseam and the outer seam and begin pressing at the hem.

> ### Note from Nancy
>
> *When you sew heavy fabrics, you may need to repeat the process or increase pressure. If this fails to produce a sharp crease, try lightly pounding the edge with a clapper. This breaks down fibers and forces them close together.*

• An "inch pinch" naturally forms at the crotch (*Diagram A*). Don't try to force this area to lie flat. Instead, allow this fold to remain at the center of the pants.

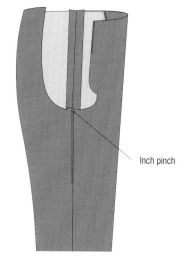

Diagram A: Inch pinch forms at crotch.

• Use a clapper to set the crease, following the same procedure as for the front crease.

Quick Technique
1.   Meet cut edges of the pants front at the hem and the crotch.
2.   Cover the fold with a press cloth; press the front crease with a steam iron.

3.   Open the pants leg, and insert a length of ThreadFuse exactly along the crease mark, on the wrong side of the fabric.

4.   Fold the leg carefully, with wrong sides together. Press from the garment right side. The thread melts, creating a sharp crease.

Pressing Darts
A dart builds shape into a garment, so press it over a similar shape.
1.   Follow these general guidelines for darts.
• Press the dart flat along the stitching line to set stitches. Stop pressing just short of the point to avoid pressing a crease.
• Place the dart over a curved surface, such as a dressmaker's ham, and press the dart to one side.

• Press vertical darts to the center.
• Press horizontal darts downward (*Diagram B*).

Diagram B: Press horizontal darts down and vertical darts toward center.

• Stop pressing ½" (1.3 cm) from dart point to avoid pressing in a dimple.
• To top-press a dart, reposition it on the ham, right side up. Cover the dart with a press cloth, and press lightly.
2.   Use the following technique to press darts in bulky fabrics, such as wools.
• Cut open the center of the dart, stopping ½" to 1" (1.3 cm to 2.5 cm) from its point.
• Press the dart flat without creasing the point.
• Insert a tapestry needle or lightweight needle in the dart point (*Diagram C*). Doing so fills out the point and prevents a dimple or ridge.

Diagram C: For heavy fabrics, insert needle in dart point.

• Place the dart over a dressmaker's ham and press. You can use a Hamholder to keep the ham in position (*Photo*). The Hamholder frees your hands for smoothing fabric during pressing.

Photo: A Hamholder keeps a dressmaker's ham upright while you press.

• Remove the needle from the dart. Top-press from the right side, covering the fabric with a press cloth.

3. Here's how to press darts in sheer or lightweight fabrics:

• Press the dart along the stitching line, taking care not to crease the edge.

• Position the dart over a dressmaker's ham. Instead of pressing the dart to one side, flatten it, placing the center of the dart underlay at the stitching line (*Diagram D*). An equal amount of the dart extends on each side of the stitching line.

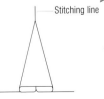

Diagram D: Center dart over stitching line in sheer fabrics.

Stitching line

Pressing Sleeves

Perfectly inserted and pressed sleeves are one mark of well-made apparel. Try these tips for shrinking out sleeve fullness and for pressing the inserted sleeve, especially when working with natural fibers.

Shrinking Sleeve Fullness with Steam

1. After easing the sleeve, match it to the armhole to see if easing is correct. If sizes correspond, steam and shape sleeve to shrink out fullness and make insertion easier.

• Position a dressmaker's ham on end with the smaller end up to simulate a shoulder shape.

• Place the wrong side of the sleeve over the ham's curved surface.

• Steam the sleeve cap. Finger-press, smoothing fabric and removing excess fullness (*Diagram E*).

Diagram E: Place sleeve over ham's curved surface; steam cap.

2. Allow the sleeve to dry on the ham to set its shape.

Pressing After Stitching Sleeve to Armhole

1. Press the seam flat. Do not press all the way to the cut edge. Press only 1/8" (3 mm) beyond the seam line to prevent flattening the cap.

2. Place the inserted sleeve on a ham so that seam allowances extend toward the sleeve cap. Press from the wrong side, using the tip of the iron and pressing only 1/8" (3 mm) beyond the seam line. This retains the sleeve's rounded shape (*Diagram F*).

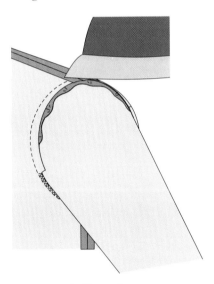

Diagram F: Place sleeve on ham and press to retain sleeve's rounded shape.

3. Allow sleeve to dry on the ham to retain its shape.

DURABLE darts

Darts are triangular folds of fabric with wide ends tapering to a point. They help shape a garment so that it fits around body contours. You can quickly sew a smooth and durable dart using the following steps:

1. Mark the dart.
• With scissors, nip the dart's stitching lines at the cut edge. On the wrong side of the garment, mark the point of the dart with a pin or a fabric marking pen.
• Fold the dart with right sides together, matching the nip markings at the cut edge.
• Mark the dart stitching line with a thread tail.
•• Place the cut edge of the fabric under the presser foot, and lower the needle but not the presser foot.
•• Pull the top thread to form an 8" to 12" (10.4 cm to 15.6 cm) thread tail. Lower the presser foot and lay the thread on top of the fabric, angling it toward the pin mark. This will mark the stitching line between the nips and the dart point (*Diagram A*).

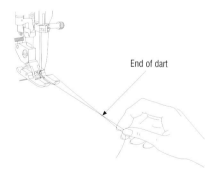
End of dart

Diagram A: Use a thread tail to mark dart stitching line.

2. Stitch the dart.
• Starting at the wide end of the dart, stitch in place several times to lock the stitching.
• Lengthen the stitch to normal length and, using the thread tail as a guide, finish stitching the dart.
• At the end of the dart, turn the machine's wheel by hand, sewing three to four stitches along the fold.
• Stitch off the fabric 1" to 2", forming a chain of thread. Secure the chained thread tail by sewing two or three stitches in place in the dart. Trim the thread ends (*Diagram B*).

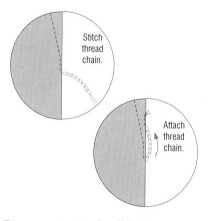
Stitch thread chain.

Attach thread chain.

Diagram B: Stitch off fabric to make thread chain; stitch thread chain to dart.

3. Press the dart. See page 86 for details on pressing.

Stitching Pleats

Think of a pleat as a minidart with no point at the end (*photo at right*). It's easy to stitch pleats using the same techniques as for darts.

1. Mark pleats using nips at ends and pen dots at tips.

2. Pin pleats, right sides together, matching nips and dots.
3. Position the edge of a piece of cardboard between the nips and dots. Attach a zipper foot. Lock stitches at the top of the pleat and stitch along the cardboard edge.
4. Press pleat underlays toward side seams (*Diagram C*). This is the opposite of pressing darts, but pressing pleats in this direction gives a more attractive appearance.

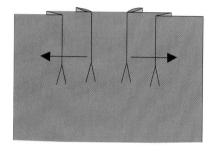

Diagram C: Press pleat underlays toward side seams.

Pleats are darts with no points at the ends.

GRACEFUL gathers

If you've ever had gathering threads break when you were nearly finished gathering a garment section, you'll appreciate my updated techniques. Most pattern guide sheets tell you to gather a skirt or other garment piece by sewing two rows of basting stitches and then pulling up the bobbin threads.

Gathering over bobbin thread or gathering with Clear Elastic is much faster than stitching two or three rows of gathering stitches. The gathering is stronger and more durable, too. The next time you need to gather a section, try one of these easy gathering methods.

But first, try changing the order in which you construct your garment.

Stitching Order

To simplify both gathering and stitching, I prefer to deviate from the usual pattern guide sheet instructions by changing the order in which I stitch the garment together.

Patterns often suggest stitching the front and back bodice sections together, then stitching the front and back skirt sections together, and finally joining the bodice to the skirt. Remember that the guide sheet is only that—a guide. I find this method easier and faster:

1. Gather the skirt front, and then stitch skirt front to bodice front.
2. Gather the skirt back, and then stitch skirt back to bodice back.
3. Join garment front to garment back at side and shoulder seams.

Gathering over Top and Bobbin Threads

The pattern guide sheet generally recommends stitching two basting rows and pulling the threads (either top or bobbin) to gather fabric. While this technique usually works, the gathering threads sometimes break.

Instead, try this method—a favorite of mine—when your pattern guide sheet calls for gathers:

1. Place the fabric under the presser foot. Turn the wheel by hand to take one complete stitch in the fabric. Bring the bobbin thread to the top by lightly pulling on the top thread. The bobbin thread will appear as a loop coming through the fabric (*Diagram A*).

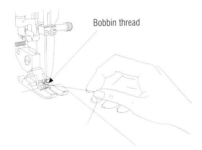

Diagram A: Pull bobbin thread to top.

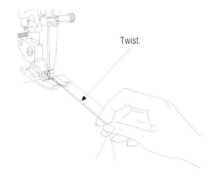

Diagram B: Gently twist threads together.

2. Pull the bobbin and top threads to measure as long as the area you plan to gather. Gently twist the two threads together (*Diagram B*).

3. Adjust your machine for a wide zigzag stitch and a short stitch length. Zigzag over the twisted threads inside the seam allowance, making a casing for the gathering threads. Make sure you don't stitch through the twisted threads (*Diagram C*).

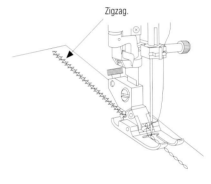

Diagram C: Zigzag over top and bobbin threads.

4. Gather by pulling the twisted threads. Because the threads are anchored in the first stitch, the gathering threads will not pull out of the fabric (*Diagram D*).

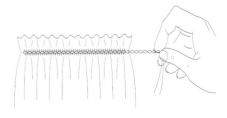

Diagram D: Gather by pulling twisted threads.

Gathering over Clear Elastic

Another option for gathering is using Clear Elastic. This unique elastic is available in ¼" and ⅜" (6 mm and 1 cm) widths. I recommend the ⅜" (1 cm) width for gathering.

Clear Elastic is lightweight yet strong and durable. It stretches to three times its length yet easily retracts to its original size. The finished gathers are even.

1.   Cut a length of ⅜" (1 cm) Clear Elastic the size of the finished garment section, including seam allowances. For example, lay the elastic on top of the bodice front pattern and use that measurement to determine the length of elastic you need to gather the front skirt section (*Diagram A*). If both front and back skirt sections are to be gathered, cut separate elastic sections for each.

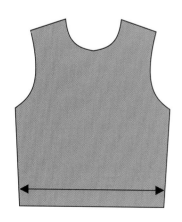

Diagram A: Measure length for Clear Elastic.

2.   Mark the garment and the elastic.
• Mark the center fronts and center backs of skirt and bodice sections with short nips.

• Mark the ⅝" (1.5 cm) seam allowances and the center on both pieces of Clear Elastic. Use a ballpoint pen for greater visibility.

Note from Nancy

I don't normally recommend ballpoint ink for transferring sewing markings, but it is one of the few things that shows clearly on this elastic. You don't have to worry about the marks showing, because the elastic is concealed once the garment is completed.

3.   Meet the elastic to the wrong side of the skirt front section, positioning its lower edge ½" (1.3 cm) from the cut edge of the fabric.
• Match and pin center markings.
• Match ends; pin elastic to garment ⅝" (1.5 cm) from each end (*Diagram B*).

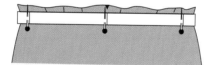

Diagram B: Pin elastic to garment, matching ends and center point.

4.   Set the sewing machine for a medium width, medium length zigzag stitch. Stitch the elastic to the garment.
• Begin sewing ⅝" (1.5 cm) from the end of the marked seam allowance.

Stretch Clear Elastic to fit as you sew.

• Stitch ½" (1.3 cm) from the cut edge of the fabric, stretching the elastic to fit (*photo*). When you complete the stitching, the elastic retracts to its original size, gathering the edge to fit the bodice front (*Diagram C*).

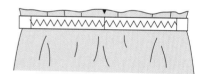

Diagram C: Zigzag Clear Elastic to waist.

5.   Stitch bodice front to skirt front, right sides together.
6.   Repeat to gather the skirt back and to stitch the bodice back to the skirt back.
7.   Stitch the side seams.

CAREFREE facings

Facings are garment pieces that cover and enclose raw edges. You may find them at necklines, armholes, or front and back openings. I've found easier ways to stitch facings than those you find in most pattern guide sheets.

Facings Applied Flat

For a quick variation, try sewing the facings to the garment sections before seaming the shoulder lines or armholes. It's so much faster to work with flat pieces than with curved pieces. You can't beat this approach when facing the tiny necklines and armholes on children's wear.

1. Fuse interfacing to the wrong sides of the front and back facings.
2. Finish the raw edges of the facings with serging, zigzagging, or Seams Great. See page 72 for information on finishing seam edges.
3. Stitch the facing to the garment, aligning the cut edges and matching notches and markings (*Diagram A*).

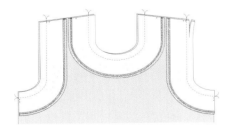

Diagram A: Stitch facings to garment.

4. Grade the seams, trimming the facing seam allowance to ¼" (6 mm).

5. Press the seams flat and then press them toward the facings.
6. Understitch, sewing the seam allowances to the facings with either a straightstitch or a multi-zigzag stitch.
7. Stitch the shoulder or underarm seams.
• Align the stitching lines of the garment front and back pieces exactly where the facings join the garment. Pin (*Diagram B*). Matching seams exactly is essential to achieve a professional look.

Diagram B: Pin garment front and back, matching seams exactly.

• Stitch continuously from the facing edge to the end of the seam. Because seam angles sometimes vary, you may need to pivot your stitching slightly when you reach the point where facing seam meets shoulder seam.

8. Press the seam allowances flat and then press them open. Trim the seam allowances of the facing section to ⅜" or 1 cm (*Diagram C*).

Diagram C: Trim seam allowance within facing section to ⅜".

9. Tack the facing to the garment.
• Turn the facing to the wrong side of the garment.
• Place the facing seam and corresponding garment seam allowances under the sewing machine needle. Be sure the garment is pushed out of the way.
• Adjust the sewing machine for a zigzag bar tack. Bar-tack through the facing and the garment seam allowances only. Do not stitch through the garment.

Matched Back Openings

Sewing a neckline facing with a back opening and center slit is a common technique, but making the back edges even can be challenging. Patterns traditionally suggest stitching the neckline and the back slit in one operation. How many times have you tried to stitch such an opening and ended up with edges of two different lengths? It's a common problem.

The next time you use a pattern that has a neckline facing with a back opening and center slit, try my updated technique. It produces superior results every time.

1. Fuse interfacing to the wrong side of the neckline facing. Finish the facing's outer edge.

2. Mark the cutting line for the back opening on both the facing and the garment back using a washable marking pen.

3. With right sides together, match seam lines and centers, and pin the facing to the neckline. Stitch around the entire neckline in one continuous seam (*Diagram A*).

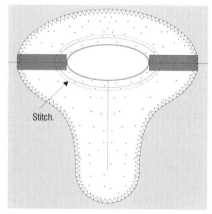

Diagram A: Stitch around entire neckline in a continuous seam.

4. Trim and grade the neckline seam allowances, trimming the facing seam allowance to approximately ¼" (6 mm) and the garment seam allowance to ⅜" (1 cm).

5. Press all seam allowances toward the facing and understitch.

6. Stitch the back opening.

• Pin the facing to the garment, stacking the back opening lines on top of each other. The neckline seam allowances wrap toward the

facing side, eliminating bulk at the neckline edge.

• Center a strip of ⅛"-wide (3 mm-wide) basting tape over the stitching line.

Note from Nancy

Basting tape is often used to "pin" slippery fabrics together. When I sew a center back facing, I use the narrowest width of basting tape, ⅛" or 3 mm, as a stitching guide. You can also cut ¼"-wide (6 mm-wide) tape in half using a rotary cutter and ruler. It's difficult to stitch lines that are exactly ⅛" apart, but with this tape, I get perfect stitching lines every time.

• Shorten your machine's stitch length to 12 to 15 stitches per inch. Stitch along both sides of the basting tape, tapering to a point at the end of the opening (*Diagram B*).

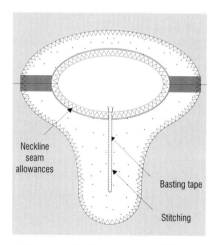

Diagram B: Center strip of basting tape over stitching line and stitch along both sides of tape.

• Remove the basting tape and cut along the back opening.

• Turn the facing to the inside and press.

Extended Jacket Facings

On most lined and unlined jackets, the front and the back facings are both approximately 3" wide at the shoulder seam. To give jackets a more professional look, extend your facing pattern pieces into the seam allowances of the sleeves. This extension gives the shoulders better shape, hides shoulder pads, and keeps facings in place.

To make a new **front facing**:

1. Pin the front facing pattern to the front jacket pattern, matching notches. Place a length of waxed or tissue paper over the pattern pieces.

2. With a felt-tip pen, extend the shoulder cutting line of the facing to the entire length of the pattern's shoulder seam and then to the center of the armhole (*Diagram C*).

3. At the center of the armhole,

Diagram C: Adjust front facing pattern.

gradually taper the cutting line back to the original facing. Cut out the new front facing pattern.

To make a new **back facing**:
1. Pin the back facing pattern to the back jacket pattern. Place waxed paper or tissue paper over the pattern pieces.
2. Make the facing shoulder seams the entire length of the jacket back shoulder seam. Extend the facing to the center of the armhole and then across to the center back. Cut out the new back facing pattern (*Diagram D*).

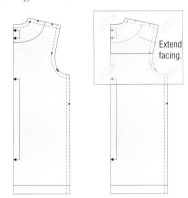

Diagram D: Extend back facing pattern to cover shoulder area.

3. If the pattern has a dart in the shoulder seam, draw the same dart on the back facing pattern. When constructing the darts, press the facing dart in the opposite direction of the jacket dart.

Facing Finishes

To prevent ravelling, finish the edges of facings. You can do this in the same way that you finish seams (see page 72), by zigzagging, serging, or edgestitching the raw edge. Or try one of the following techniques for a more professional-looking edge:
1. Seams Great, a notion made of ⅝"-wide (1.5 cm-wide) nylon fabric, neatly binds a raw edge without adding bulk. It's cut on the bias and will mold around the curves of the outer edge of facings. Place the raw edge of the fabric within the curl of the Seams Great, and straightstitch or zigzag in place (*Diagram E*).

Diagram E: Finish raw edge with Seams Great.

2. Serge the raw edge by using a 2- or a 3-thread overedge stitch.
3. Bind the edges with a bias strip of fabric (*Diagram F*).

Diagram F: Finish raw edge with bias trim.

• Cut 1"-wide (2.5 cm-wide) bias strips from a lightweight blouse or dress fabric that coordinates with the jacket fabric.
• With right sides together and raw edges aligned, place the bias strips on the facing or seam edge. Stitch using a ¼" (6 mm) seam allowance.
• Wrap the bias strip around the raw edge of the facing to the underside of the fabric. You don't have to finish the unsewn edge of the strip, because the bias edge won't ravel.
• Stitch in-the-ditch (the groove of the seam) to catch the underside of the strip (*Diagram G*).

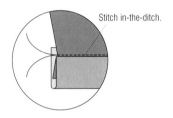

Diagram G: Stitch in-the-ditch to catch underside of bias strip.

Note from Nancy

To "stitch in-the-ditch" means to stitch from the right side in the groove or "ditch" of the seam. The stitching line is hidden in the seam, yet it catches the underside of the fabric. You'll find many other areas where stitching in-the-ditch works well.

Eliminating Facings

Sometimes the best way to simplify sewing facings is to eliminate them completely. When sewing sleeveless children's clothes, such as jumpers and vests, facings can add a lot of bulk in the shoulder area.

You can eliminate this extra bulk by finishing the edge with a binding rather than a facing. This technique works whether you're sewing with woven fabric or knits.

To eliminate facings on **woven fabrics**:

1. Trim the entire armhole and neckline seam allowances on the main garment pieces (*Diagram A*). The armhole and neckline of the trimmed pieces are now finished size.

Diagram A: Trim seam allowances.

2. Cut 2"-wide (5.4 cm-wide) bias strips of matching or contrasting fabric the length of the armhole and neckline edges.

3. Clean-finish one long edge of each strip by zigzagging or serging.

Note from Nancy

Because the fabric strips are cut on the bias, a finish is not absolutely necessary, since a bias edge won't ravel. However, for durability and appearance, especially on children's clothes, I like to zigzag or serge this edge.

4. Stitch bias strips to the neckline and armhole openings.
• Place right sides together.
• Pin bias to openings, molding the strips around neckline and armhole curves.
• Stitch strips to garment openings with ³⁄₈" or ½" (1 cm or 1.3 cm) seams (*Diagram B*). This width provides an attractive finished binding

on most children's clothing. If you're sewing clothes for an adult, adjust the width of the seam to suit your taste. Remember to adjust the width of the bias strip accordingly. Cut the strip approximately four times the width of the finished binding.

Diagram B: Stitch bias strips to neckline and armhole openings.

5. Fold bias strips up to cover the raw edge; press.
6. Wrap the bias strip to the wrong side of the garment, enclosing the raw edge. Measure carefully to be sure the part of the binding that shows on the garment's right side is the same width on the entire garment. Press.
7. Secure the bias strip by stitching in-the-ditch from the right side of the garment. This technique is similar to a Hong Kong finish. You can also secure the bias strip by topstitching.

To eliminate facings on **knit fabrics**:
1. Trim armhole and neckline seam allowances as indicated in Step 1 for woven fabrics.
2. Using ribbing or matching or contrasting knit fabric, cut 2"-wide (5 cm-wide) binding strips on the crosswise grain. The crosswise grain on knits has a great deal of stretch, so take advantage of it when you bind knit edges.
3. Pin the ribbing or knit binding to the armhole and neckline, right sides together, slightly stretching

the binding to meet the main fabric. Stitch the binding to the garment with ³⁄₈" or ½" (1 cm or 1.3 cm) seam allowances.
4. Wrap the binding to the wrong side. Measure so that the entire binding is the same width.
5. Secure the ribbing to the garment in one of these ways:
• Topstitch with a decorative stretch stitch, working from the right side of the garment (*Diagram C*).

Diagram C: Use decorative stretch stitching (left) or double-needle stitching (right) to sew ribbing to garment.

Note from Nancy

Sometimes the edges of single knits roll and curl toward the right side of the fabric. This can make it difficult to stitch an even binding around an armhole or neckline opening. If your knit edges curl, zigzag or serge the binding to the garment rather than straight-stitching the seam.

• For a more tailored finish, insert a double needle and stitch along the binding (*Diagram C*). See page 64 for information on sewing with a double needle.

waistbands

Some people avoid buying patterns with separate waistbands because they find the finished garment has too much bulk at the waist. **If that has happened to you, try my waistband technique.** It eliminates bulk by removing part of the seam allowance before you cut the band. Here's how to do it:

1. Cut out the waistband.

• Fold under ½" (1.3 cm) along the long unnotched edge of the waistband pattern (*Diagram A*).

Diagram A: Fold under ½" along unnotched edge of waistband pattern.

• Align the folded edge of the waistband pattern along the fabric selvage, if possible. The selvage provides a neat, ravel-free edge. If you can't place the band on the selvage, finish the edge by zigzagging or serging.

• Cut out the pattern, marking notches and centers.

2. Interface the waistband.

• Fuse interfacing to the wrong side of the waistband.

Note from Nancy

Jiffy Waistband & Ban-Rol makes interfacing waistbands even easier. Available in a 1¼" (3.2 cm) finished width, it has perforated stitching and fold lines that serve as positioning guides. You'll get uniform waistbands every time!

• To use Jiffy Waistband & Ban-Rol, place the fusible side to the wrong side of the waistband, positioning the center slot along the fold line. Cover with a damp press cloth, and fuse for 15 seconds with the iron temperature set on wool.

3. Stitch the waistband to the garment, right sides together, matching notches and centers. The waistband will extend beyond the garment on each end.

4. Grade the seam allowances.

• Trim the waistband seam to ¼" (6 mm).

• Trim the garment seam to ⅜" (1 cm).

• Cut skirt seam allowances and darts at an angle by trimming from the stitching line to the cut edge to reduce bulk (*Diagram B*).

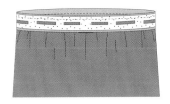

Diagram B: Stitch, grade, and angle-cut darts and seam allowances.

4. Press seam flat; then press waistband up, covering the seam.

5. Stitch the ends of the band.

• Fold band along the center slot, right sides together, meeting cut ends. Lower edges will not meet; the selvage or finished edge extends ⅛" (3 mm) below the other edge.

• Stitch ⅝" (1.5 cm) from the cut edges of the waistband.

•• On the left end, stitch straight up from the zipper overlap.

•• On the right end, let a portion of the waistband extend past the zipper, creating an underlap (*Diagram C*).

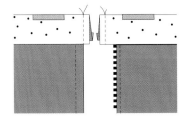

Diagram C: On the right end, a portion of the waistband extends beyond the zipper.

• Trim and grade seam; angle-cut corners.

• Turn band ends right side out. Use a Bamboo Pointer & Creaser to get sharp corners.

6. Stitch in-the-ditch along the remaining waistband edge.

• Pin the selvage or finished edge of the waistband to the skirt, covering waistline seam. Pin from the right side of the garment. The fold line will be at the top of the band, and the selvage or finished edge of the band will extend ⅛" (3 mm) below the waistline seam.

• Stitch in-the-ditch from the right side of the garment. Stitches will catch and secure the ⅛" (3 mm) extension.

Fit-and-Stretch Waistband

For a waistband that looks like a fitted band but has the comfort of a stretchable waistband, use elastic instead of interfacing. Here's how:

1. Prepare the waistband.

• Cut a new waistband pattern 3½" (9 cm) wide and the length of the garment waistline, plus 2" (5 cm) for the seam allowance and underlay extension.

• Clean-finish one lengthwise edge by zigzagging or serging or by using Seams Great.

• Mark the lengthwise fold line, 1⅝" (4 cm) from the clean-finished edge. Fold with wrong sides together and press (*Diagram A*).

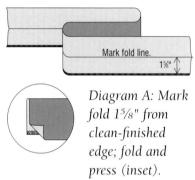

Diagram A: Mark fold 1⅝" from clean-finished edge; fold and press (inset).

2. Insert the zipper in the garment.

3. Join the waistband to the garment.

• Pin the unfinished edge of the waistband to the garment, right sides together, extending the waistband ⅝" (1.5 cm) beyond the lapped (left) side of the zipper opening. On the underlap (right) side, the waistband extends approximately 1½" (3.8 cm) beyond the zipper opening.

• Stitch the waistband to the waistline with a ⅝" (1.5 cm) seam (*Diagram B*).

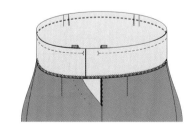

Diagram B: Stitch waistband to skirt.

• Grade the seam allowances, and press the waistband and the seam allowances up.

4. Add elastic to the waistline.

• Fold the waistband along the fold line, right sides together.

• Place 1"-wide (2.5 cm-wide) no-roll elastic on top of the waistband, cutting the elastic slightly longer than the waistband.

• Pin one end of the elastic at the waistline center back seam, with raw edges even. Stitch, catching the elastic in the seam. Stitch a second time (*Diagram C*).

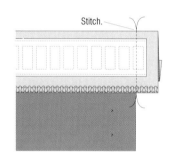

Diagram C: Stitch elastic to waistband end.

• Grade the seam allowance and angle-cut the corner.

• Place a bodkin, a safety pin, or an Elastic Glide on the free end of the elastic to prevent the elastic from twisting.

• Turn the waistband to the right side, encasing the elastic. The waistband facing will extend about ¼" (6 mm) beyond the stitching line. Press the waistband to the 1¼" (3.2 cm) finished size.

5. Working from the garment's right side, stitch in-the-ditch in the waistband seam to attach the underside of the waistband. The elastic still floats inside the waistband.

6. Fit the garment.

• Pull the elastic to the correct tightness.

• Pin through all the layers at the underlap extension, and cut off excess elastic.

7. Finish the waistband.

• Zigzag or satin-stitch the unfinished end of the waistband, sewing through all the layers, including the elastic.

• Trim off any excess elastic or fabric whiskers.

• Stitch a decorative box on both the lapped and the underlapped sides of the waistband to keep the elastic flat at the closure (*Diagram D*).

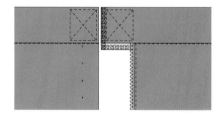

Diagram D: Stitch decorative box at both waistband ends.

• Sew on buttons or hooks and eyes as desired.

Zip-to-the-Top Waistband

When you have a skirt pattern that fits well, the Zip-to-the-Top Waistband can speed your sewing. Whether you make the waistband narrow or wide, the zipper extends to the top of the band, eliminating the need for a button or hook-and-eye closure.
1. Modify the waistband pattern.
• For a 1¼"-wide (3.2 cm-wide) finished waistband, cut the width of the waistband 3½" (9 cm) wide. Use the waistband pattern piece to cut the length, allowing ⅝" (1.5 cm) seam allowances at the center back.
• Cut out the waistband pattern piece with the unnotched lengthwise edge along the selvage. If you have two raw edges, clean-finish the unnotched edge after applying the interfacing (see Step 2).

Note from Nancy

With this technique, the unnotched edge of the band is exposed inside the skirt. When cutting out the waistband pattern, align the unnotched edge with the selvage of the fabric, if possible. Presto! The edge is finished.

• Place ¼" (6 mm) clips in the waistband at each notch and other pattern markings (*Diagram E*).

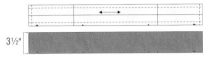

3½"

Diagram E: Modify waistband pattern.

2. Prepare the waistband.
• Fold the waistband with wrong sides together, allowing the notched edge to extend ⅜" (1 cm) beyond the unnotched edge.
• Interface the waistband using Jiffy Waistband & Ban-Rol. Fuse the interfacing to the wrong side of the waistband (*Diagram F*).

Interfacing

Diagram F: Fuse interfacing to waistband.

• Clean-finish the unnotched edge if you did not cut it out on the selvage.
3. Stitch the waistband to the skirt.
• Stitch the darts or the pleats in the front and back skirt sections.
• Stitch the skirt front to the skirt back at the side seams, leaving the center back seam unstitched.
• Pin the waistband to the skirt, right sides together. Stitch, using a ⅝" (1.5 cm) seam allowance.
• Grade the seam allowances, cutting the waistband seam allowance narrower than the skirt seam allowance. Press the seam toward the waistband.

4. Stitch the center back seam of the skirt and the waistband. Use a machine basting stitch in the zipper area. Stop stitching at the waistband fold line. Press the seam open (*Diagram G*).

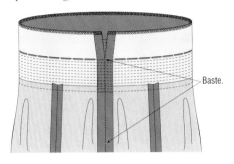

Baste.

Diagram G: Baste zipper opening to waistband fold.

5. Follow the instructions on page 119 to insert a centered zipper.
• Buy a zipper 2" (5 cm) longer than the zipper opening to extend the zipper into the waistband.
• Insert the zipper, positioning the zipper stop at the waistband fold line. Topstitch the zipper in place.
6. Secure the waistband edges.
• Fold under the unstitched edges of the waistband, covering the zipper tape. Handstitch the band to the zipper.
• Working from the wrong side, pin the lengthwise waistband edge in place.
• Stitch in-the-ditch from the right side along the lower waistband edge, securing the unsewn waistband facing seam allowance.

collars

To eliminate bulk from a collar, sew the outer edges in three steps. I call this the "wrapped-corner technique," and it ranks as one of my favorites. You, too, will be pleased with the great-looking results, which you can accomplish in minutes.

Patterns for tailored shirts, blouses, and jackets generally include pieces for both upper and under collars. Casual-wear patterns, however, usually provide only one pattern piece for the collar. The following instructions are for patterns with upper and under collars, but you can use this technique even if your pattern has only one collar piece.

Most guide sheet instructions call for interfacing only one collar layer—the under collar when separate pieces are given, and the half of the collar closest to the neckline when a single piece is given. But interfacing both the upper and under collar adds body and makes the collar seam stronger. Use a lightweight interfacing, such as Pellon's featherweight to midweight fusible interfacing.

The wrapped-corner technique makes stitching collars easy.

1. Cut out fusible interfacing for both collar pieces. Fuse the interfacing to the wrong sides of the collar pieces.
2. With right sides together, pin the upper and under collars together along the unnotched edge. Stitch the seam from end to end.
3. Press the seam to one side and then press it open.
4. Grade the under collar seam allowance to ¼" (6 mm) and the upper collar seam allowance to ⅜" (1 cm).
5. Press the seam allowances toward the under collar and understitch the entire seam (*Diagram A*).

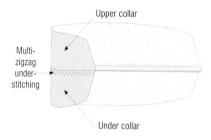

Diagram A: Understitch seam joining under collar to upper collar.

Note from Nancy

When I sew medium-weight or heavier fabric, I like to use a multizigzag stitch for the understitching. It gives more stitches per inch than a regular zigzag, creating a crisper collar edge. If your sewing machine doesn't have a multizigzag stitch, use a regular zigzag.

6. Fold the collar along the seam, with right sides together. The seam

allowances will roll toward the under collar. Stitch from the fold to the neckline edge (*Diagram B*).

Diagram B: Fold collar along seam and stitch from fold to neckline edge.

7. To reduce bulk, grade the seam allowances, trimming the corners at an angle. Press the seams to one side and then press them open. Press the corners over a point presser.
8. Turn the collar right side out and machine-baste the open edges together. Press.

Classic Peter Pan Collar

A Peter Pan collar is a feature often found on blouses and dresses, especially those designed for children. There's nothing more distracting than having the under collar roll to the right side, as it sometimes does. Here are tips to prevent the problem:

1. Prepare the collar.
• Cut four collar pieces (two of the upper collar and two of the under collar), and interface them all.
• Trim ⅛" (3 mm) from the outer, unnotched edges of the under collar pieces, but don't trim the neck edge. Trimming is essential to keeping the under collar from rolling to the upper side.
• With right sides together and the outer edges aligned, pin one upper collar piece to one under collar piece

to make one half-collar. Repeat this step for the remaining collar pieces.

2. Stitch the collar pieces together.

• Stitch with the under collar next to the presser foot and the upper collar next to the feed dogs. This automatically eases the upper collar to fit the smaller under collar. Press the seam to one side.

Note from Nancy

Whenever you sew together two fabric pieces of different lengths, stitch with the longer layer down (next to the feed dogs of the sewing machine) and the shorter layer up (next to the presser foot). The feed dogs will gently and evenly ease the longer layer to fit the shorter layer.

• Grade the seam, trimming the under collar seam allowances to ¼" (6 mm) and the upper collar seam allowances to ⅜" (1 cm) (*Diagram C*).

Diagram C: Grade seam allowances.

• Turn the collar right side out and press.

Note from Nancy

For a pressing template, use a lightweight piece of cardboard cut to the shape of the pattern piece (without seam allowances). You can also use the Pocket Curve Template. Although it's generally used to make round curves on patch pockets, this notion can do double duty as a template for the curved Peter Pan collar.

• Working from the right side, understitch the seam, sewing all the seam allowances to the under collar (*Diagram D*). Press.

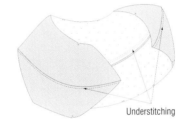

Understitching

Diagram D: Understitch from right side, sewing all seam allowances to under collar.

3. Apply the collar to the garment, following the guide sheet instructions.

Blouse Collar and Collar Band

This technique eliminates the bulk from the center front seams and automatically places the under collar on the bias to give the collar greater shape.

1. Create a new collar pattern.

• Cut the pattern apart at the center back (*Diagram E*).

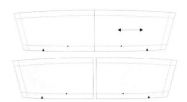

Diagram E: Cut apart collar pattern at center back.

• Fold under the seam allowance of the center front of one collar, and align it with the stitching line of the other collar center front (*Diagram F*). Pin. Trim the extra triangle shape that forms when you overlap the collar sections.

Diagram F: Fold under seam allowance. Meet stitching lines.

• Place waxed paper over the pattern and trace the new collar outline. Add a ⅝" (1.5 cm) seam allowance to one end of the new pattern (*Diagram G*). Write "place on fold" at the other end, and cut out the new pattern piece.

Add ⅝"

Center
Place on fold.

Diagram G: Add ⅝" seam.

2. Position the new pattern on the fabric fold and cut out the collar.

3. Using the new pattern, cut out interfacing and fuse it to the wrong side of the collar (*Diagram A*).

Diagram A: Fuse interfacing to collar.

Note from Nancy

If you're working with a stripe fabric, refold the fabric so that its grain runs horizontally on the upper collar. If you're sewing with a plain fabric, grain placement is less critical. I've made collars using either grain line, and both placements work fine.

4. Sew the center back seam and press.

5. Sew the outer edge.

• Refold the collar, with right sides together and the seam placed at the center back.

• Stitch the outer edge (*Diagram B*).

Diagram B: Center seam and stitch outer collar edge.

• Press the seam flat and then open. Grade the seam allowances, trimming the under collar seam to ¼" (6 mm). Trim the collar points

on the diagonal to eliminate bulk.

6. To understitch, use a multi-zigzag stitch, sewing all seam allowances to the under collar to within 1" (2.5 cm) of the collar points (*Diagram C*). If your machine doesn't have this stitch, use a regular zigzag.

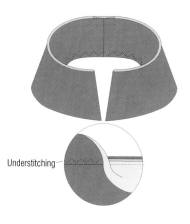

Diagram C: Understitch collar.

7. Turn the collar right side out and press.

Note from Nancy

You can instantly turn collar and lapel points with a Collar Point & Tube Turner. Place the collar between the scissorlike prongs, with the rounded point of the turner on the inside of the collar, and turn the collar right side out. The pointed end helps form the point of the collar.

Collar Band

When I first began sewing, I used to avoid patterns with collar bands because the center front curves

always had a lump caused by the bulk of the seams. This changed when I learned a bulk-free collar band technique. Combine it with the collar technique explained at left for your next tailored blouse project.

1. Update the pattern pieces.

• Extend the notches toward the seam line.

• To prepare the pattern pieces for a ¼" (6 mm) seam, trim ⅜" (1 cm) from the neck edges of the front and back pieces and the collar band (*Diagram D*).

Diagram D: Trim ⅜" from neck edge of front, back, and collar band.

• Keep in mind that a ¼" (6 mm) seam isn't very wide. Be sure to practice sewing these narrow seams on your machine before stitching them on your garment.

• Mark the collar bands at the large dots along the collar edge using a fabric marking pen or pencil.

2. Cut out interfacing pieces and fuse them to both collar bands.

3. Place the collar bands with right sides together and sandwich the neckline in between. Sew the three layers together along the neckline with a ¼" (6 mm) seam (*Diagram E*).

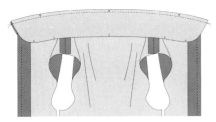

Diagram E: Sandwich neckline between collar bands.

4. Stitch the curve of the collar band.

• Mark the stopping point for the curved corner with a nip.

• Roll the center fronts into cone shapes until the fabric is next to the neckline seam and the collar bands align, right sides together (*Diagram F*).

• Wrap the neckline seam allowances down toward the inside band.

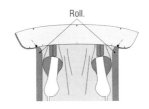

Diagram F: Roll center fronts into cones.

• Stitch the curve of the collar band from the fold to the mark (*Diagram G*).

Diagram G: Stitch from folded edge to nip.

• Turn the collar band to the right side, and check to see if the curve is smooth. If it is, turn the collar wrong side out and restitch the curve with 18 to 20 stitches per inch.

5. Clip to the seam allowance at the mark and grade seams to ⅛" (3 mm).

6. Turn the neckband right side out and press (*Diagram H*).

Diagram H: Turn neckband right side out.

7. Attach the collar and finish the collar band.

• Pin the right side of the completed collar to the inner collar band. Stitch with a ⅝" (1.5 cm) seam (*Diagram I*).

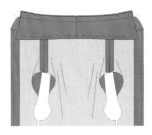

Diagram I: Pin collar to inner collar band and stitch.

• Grade and press the seam allowances.

8. Fold under the outer collar band seam allowance. Pin the outer collar band over the collar and edgestitch around the band (*Diagram J*).

Diagram J: Edgestitch collar band.

Stitching a Notched Collar for a Jacket

It's easy to stitch a notched collar on a jacket. Here's how:

1. Machine-baste the collar to the neckline, using a ½" (1.3 cm) seam allowance (*Diagram A*).

Diagram A: Machine-baste collar to neckline.

2. Pin front facings to back facing at shoulders and stitch (*Diagram B*).

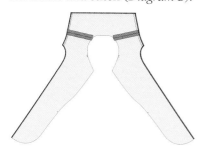

Diagram B: Join front and back facing at shoulders.

3. Pin the facing piece to the jacket neckline, with right sides together and raw edges aligned, and stitch (*Diagram C*). Press the seam flat and then open.

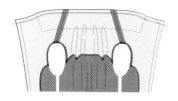

Diagram C: Pin facing to jacket neckline and stitch.

4. Grade the seam allowance, cutting the facing edge shorter.

5. Press the seam allowance toward the facing, and understitch only between the shoulder seams of the back facing (*Diagram D*).

Understitch.

Diagram D: Understitch back facing.

6. Stitch the lapel corner.

• At the lapel corner, wrap the neckline seam allowance toward the jacket side (*Diagram E*). The stitching line for the neckline will be at the fold. Pin.

Diagram E: Wrap corner on lapel.

Note from Nancy

Wrapping corners is not just for collars and lapels. Any time you stitch a corner, you can wrap the seam allowances to one side to get a sharp, crisp corner. Wrapping corners also eliminates the need to stop and pivot at corners.

• Pin the facing to the jacket along the center edges, matching notches.

(The facing is generally ¼" or 6 mm longer than the jacket front, so that the facing will fit smoothly as it becomes the turned-back lapel.)

• Stitch the front seam with the jacket side up.

• Press the seam flat and then open. Grade and angle-cut the bulk from the lapel point, as illustrated (*Diagram F*).

Diagram F: Grade seam; angle-cut lapel point.

• Clip to the stitching line at the end of the lapel roll line, across from the top buttonhole position (*Diagram G*).

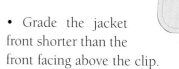

Diagram G: Clip to stitching line at end of lapel roll line.

• Grade the jacket front shorter than the front facing above the clip.

• Grade the front facing shorter than the jacket front below the clip.

• Press the seam allowance below the clip toward the facing and understitch.

• Press the seam allowance above the clip toward the jacket front and understitch.

7. Turn the collar and the lapel right side out and press.

Set-in sleeves are a common feature of many garments, and they can vary widely depending on styling. A sleeve may be short, long, cuffed, uncuffed, lined, or unlined. You may need only to ease the sleeve cap slightly to get it to fit the armscye (armhole opening), or the style may call for a fully gathered sleeve.

Sleeve Easing

To ease a sleeve cap, I was taught to sew two rows of basting threads and then draw them up. This technique certainly works, but it can be frustrating if the basting threads break or create puckers.

Here are four other options for easing sleeve caps. Experiment with these choices for the best results in the least amount of time.

Eraser easing uses two pencils with erasers to ease the fullness from the sleeve cap. I think you'll find that eraser easing is faster and more accurate than traditional basted easing.

• Place the sleeve under the presser foot at one of the notches. Lower the needle into the fabric, about 1/2" (1.3 cm) from the edge of the fabric.

• Place one pencil eraser on the fabric on each side of the presser foot, directly in front of the needle (*Diagram A*).

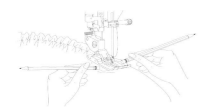

Diagram A: Use pencil erasers to ease sleeves.

• Pull the erasers outward, away from the presser foot, as you stitch around the sleeve cap, forcing the fabric to stretch on the bias. Stitch a small section and reposition the erasers. Continue stitching to the next notch.

Finger easing requires only one row of stitching between notches and is perfect for lightweight to medium-weight fabrics. If you haven't tried this technique before, practice on a fabric scrap until you get the hang of it.

• Adjust the stitching length according to the fabric weight: 10–12 for medium weight; and 12–14 for lightweight.

• Stitch 1/2" (1.3 cm) from the curved edge of the sleeve.

• Firmly press your finger against the back of the presser foot. Stitch 2" to 3", trying to stop the fabric from flowing behind the presser foot; release your finger and repeat. Your finger will prevent the flow of fabric from behind the presser foot, causing the feed dogs to ease each stitch slightly (*Photo A*).

Photo A: Press your finger against the back of the presser foot for finger easing.

• If you have eased too much, simply snip a stitch or two to release some of the gathers. Pull a thread if you need to gather more.

Seams Great easing uses this brand-name seam finisher to ease sleeves on lightweight to medium-weight fabrics (*Photo B*). Buy the wider 1 1/4" (3.2 cm) width for easing. This is the perfect easing option for a beginner.

Photo B: Seams Great is a bias-cut nylon seam finish.

• Pin the front and back patterns together at the shoulder seams, stacking the stitching lines. Measure the stitching line from the front notch to the back notch. Cut the 1 1/4"-wide (3.2 cm-wide) Seams Great the length of the armhole measurement, plus 1" (2.5 cm) for handles.

Note from Nancy

When I use Seams Great, I like to have a 1/2" (1.3 cm) handle on each end to hold while stretching the Seams Great to meet the sleeve. I use this same handle idea when easing with Clear Elastic.

• Measure ½" (1.3 cm) from each end and mark with a pin. Mark the center, too. Pin the Seams Great to the wrong side of the sleeve with three pins, matching the raw edges at the notches and cap.

• Grasp the handles of the Seams Great, and stretch it until it fits the area between the notches. Sew both layers together ½" (1.3 cm) from the cut edge using a regular stitch length. The Seams Great will retract to its original size, easing the sleeve.

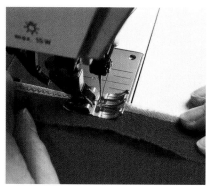

Photo A: Seams Great is great for gathering light-weight and medium-weight fabrics.

Clear Elastic easing uses ⅜"-wide (1 cm-wide) Clear Elastic to ease sleeves in bulky woven and knit fabrics.

• Pin the front and the back patterns together at the shoulder seam, stacking the stitching lines. Measure the length of the armhole along the seam line, from the front notch and across the shoulder to the back notch.

• Cut Clear Elastic the length of the armhole measurement plus 1" for handles.

• Measure ½" (1.3 cm) from each end and mark with a ballpoint pen. Fold the elastic in half and mark the center. Mark the positions for the top of the sleeve cap (shoulder) and the sleeve dots, too.

• Set your machine to a medium stitch length.

• With the elastic on the wrong side of the fabric, align the marks on the elastic with the notches, the sleeve dots, and the shoulders.

• Sew a few stitches at one sleeve notch to anchor the elastic to the sleeve. Stretch the elastic to meet the sleeve and stitch, beginning and ending at the notches and using the handle to stretch the elastic.

• You don't need to remove the elastic; it doesn't add any bulk.

Setting in Sleeves

Most pattern guide sheets provide clear instructions for inserting the sleeve style that pattern calls for. However, I've found some shortcuts for various types of sleeve insertions. With some styles, you get a more professional look if you take a little time to add pieces such as sleeve heads and sleeve boosters.

Here's the basic technique for setting in a sleeve:

1. Pin the sleeve cap to the armhole. Distribute ease evenly in the armscye, matching notches and circles.

2. Sew the sleeve into the armhole.

• Stitch all the way around, with the sleeve on top to control the distribution of the fabric.

Diagram A: Stitch entire armhole; then stitch underarm area again.

• Restitch the underarm between the notches, using a ⅜" (1 cm) seam allowance (*Diagram A*).

• Trim the underarm seam to the second stitching. This makes the sleeve fit better. Zigzag or serge the edge to prevent ravelling.

3. Press the armhole seam. This is extremely important. Proper pressing gives a smoother appearance.

• Press the seam flat, but don't press it open.

• Press all seam allowances toward the sleeve, away from the garment. To help build shape into the sleeve, press it over a dressmaker's ham. The ham is shaped and curved like the armhole.

• Always press on the wrong side.

Adding a Sleeve Booster

When your sleeve pattern features pleats or gathers, give the design feature staying power with a sleeve booster. A sleeve booster is a type of sleeve head sewn into garments to keep the gathers or pleats pronounced (*Photo B, page 105*).

For woven fabrics, use a double layer of organza or bridal illusion (veiling fabric); for knit tops, consider using a single layer of polyester fleece.

Photo B: Use organza to make a sleeve booster for woven fabrics.

Here's how to do it:

1. Place a piece of waxed paper or tissue paper over the cap of the sleeve pattern and outline the cap. Measure 2" (3.1 cm) down from the center dot, and taper this line to the dots on either side of the sleeve (*Diagram B*).

Diagram B: Measure 2" from shoulder seam dot.

2. Use the cap pattern to cut the supportive fabrics. Zigzag, serge, or use ⅝"-wide (1.5 cm-wide) Seams Great to clean-finish the raw edges (*Diagram C*).

Seams Great

Diagram C: Use Seams Great to clean-finish raw edges.

3. Pin the sleeve booster fabric to the wrong side of the sleeve. Gather or pleat the sleeve and the sleeve booster as one.

4. Set in the sleeve. The added fabric keeps the gathers pronounced, even through washings.

Fold-and-Stitch Hems

You can hem short sleeves in minutes using this quick technique. The hem edge is hidden inside the tuck and remains durable and ravel-free for the life of the garment. For easier maneuvering, hem the sleeve before setting it into the armhole.

1. Stitch the underarm seam of the sleeve. Press the seam to one side and then press it open.

2. Clip the seam allowances to the stitching at the hemline. Then trim the seam allowances to ¼" (6 mm), from the hemline to the lower edge of the sleeve (*Diagram D*).

Diagram D: Trim seam allowances to ¼" from hemline to sleeve lower edge.

3. Fold up the hem allowance and press. Fold up the hem allowance again. Press.

4. Stitch ¼" (6 mm) from the second fold, catching the raw edge of the hem and creating a tuck

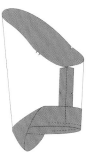

Diagram E: Stitch ¼" from second fold.

Diagram F: Turn hem down and tuck up; press.

(*Diagram E*). Turn the hem down and the tuck up; press (*Diagram F*).

Quick Lined Sleeves

Stitching a lined sleeve can be just as fast as sewing an unlined one. My method automatically hems the sleeve as you line it. It can even create an accent if you turn back the sleeve to show off a contrasting lining. The lining gives the sleeve additional body and makes it easier to slip on over a blouse or a sweater.

To line a sleeve:

1. Cut the lining.

Note from Nancy

Because you line and hem this sleeve at the same time, it's important to alter the sleeve to the correct length before you cut out the pattern. Double-check your arm length against the pattern's sleeve length and make any needed changes.

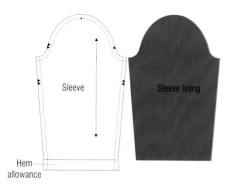

Diagram A: Fold under hem allowance on pattern.

• Fold under the hem allowance on the sleeve pattern to create the lining pattern (*Diagram A*).
• Cut out the lining.
2.   Join the sleeve and the lining at the hem edge.
• Align the hem edges of the sleeve and the sleeve lining, right sides together, and pin. Stitch using a ⅝" (1.5 cm) seam (*Diagram B*).

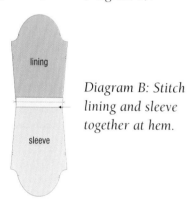

Diagram B: Stitch lining and sleeve together at hem.

3.   Grade the hem seam allowance, making the lining seam the smallest. Press the seam flat and then towards the lining.
4.   Stitch the underarm seam.
• With right sides together, align and pin the underarm seams of the lining and the sleeve.
• Stitch the entire underarm seam

Diagram C: Stitch underarm seam.

(*Diagram C*). Press the seam flat and then open, pressing over a seam roll or a Seam Stick.
5.   Complete the sleeve lining.
• Reach inside the fashion fabric sleeve, grasp the fashion fabric and lining at the hemline, and pull the

Diagram D: Meet raw edges of sleeve and lining at sleeve cap; zigzag or serge edges together.

sleeve right side out.
• Align the raw edges of the sleeve and the lining at the sleeve cap (*Diagram D*).
• Smooth out the sleeve hem and press.
• Zigzag or serge sleeve caps together, handling the two sleeve layers as one.
6.   Ease the fullness in the sleeve cap using Clear Elastic. See page 104

Note from Nancy

I think the armhole seam of a jacket needs the shape of the sleeve head to fill out the fullness of the cap. By waiting to press the seam toward the sleeve after the sleeve head is in place, you avoid pressing wrinkles into the sleeve.

for how to do Clear Elastic easing.
7.   Set in the sleeve, waiting to press until after you add a sleeve head.
8.   Add a sleeve head (see below).

Adding a Sleeve Head

After you set the sleeve in a jacket, insert a sleeve head. This small strip of fleece helps fill out the fullness of the cap, for a softer, more professional appearance.
1.   Cut two strips of polyester fleece each 1½" x 10" (3.8 cm x 25.5 cm). Fold each strip in half and mark the center.
2.   Align the raw edges of the sleeve cap and the straight edge of the sleeve head. Match the center mark with the shoulder seam and pin (*Diagram E*).

Diagram E: Align sleeve head with armhole/sleeve edges; pin.

3.   Working from the jacket side of the armhole, stitch the sleeve head in place, sewing over the previous stitching.
4.   With the wrong side out, press the seam over a dressmaker's ham. Press the seam allowances and the sleeve head toward the sleeve.

CUSTOM-MADE shoulder pads

Shoulder pads give a special finishing touch to the shoulder and the sleeve area. They make your jacket hang correctly from the shoulders for a flattering look.

You can buy shoulder pads, but it's easy and economical to make your own. By tracing the shoulder shape of the front and the back pattern pieces, you can make a pair of custom-fitted shoulder pads. Here's how to do it:

1. Prepare the pattern.
• Stack the shoulder stitching lines of the front and the back pattern pieces.
• Place three sheets of waxed paper over the shoulder area.
• Trace the armhole cutting line between the dots and the shoulder seam using a dull pencil or a tracing wheel (*Diagram A*).

Diagram A: Trace shoulder seam and armhole cutting line.

2. Draw the shoulder pad shapes.
• Place a pin at the armhole edge of the shoulder seam cutting line. Tape thread or string to a felt-tip pen; wind the other end around the pin several times until the length of the thread between the pin and the pen point is 5" (12.5 cm).

Diagram B: Draw arc, beginning and ending at armhole edges.

Draw an arc, beginning and ending at the armhole edges (*Diagram B*).

Note from Nancy

Using a Yardstick Compass is the quickest way to draw arcs. Insert a 12" (30.5 cm) ruler between the components of the Yardstick Compass. Make the space between the pointed end of the compass and the pencil end equal to the length of the shoulder seam (minus the seam allowances). Draw two smaller arcs in the same manner, moving the pen to decrease the space 1" (2.5 cm) each time.

• Move the pen in 1" (2.5 cm) toward the armhole edges, and wind the thread around the pin until taut. Draw a second arc, 1" (2.5 cm) smaller than the previous arc.
• Move the pen in 1" (2.5 cm) and repeat to complete the third arc (*Diagram C*).

3. Cut the shapes.
• Cut four layers of fusible interfac-

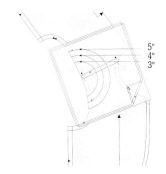

Diagram C: Draw 5" arc; draw 4" arc; draw 3" arc.

ing using the largest arc pattern.
• Cut two layers each of thick fusible craft fleece using the two smaller arc patterns.
• Make nips on all the pads at the inner and the outer shoulder seams for easy alignment (*Diagram D*).

4. Create the shoulder pad.
• Stand a pressing ham on its side. Place one layer of fusible interfacing on it, fusible side up.

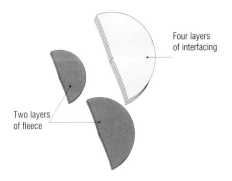

Four layers of interfacing

Two layers of fleece

Diagram D: Make nips on all pads.

• Center a piece of the smallest arc of fleece on top of the fusible layer; then center the remaining arc of fleece over the smallest piece,

matching nips.
• Top the layers with a layer of fusible interfacing, with the fusible side down.
• Place pins along the center of the shoulder pad, and smooth the layers around the pressing ham so that the shoulder pad conforms to the ham (*photo below*).

Pin center of shoulder pad and shape it on a dressmaker's ham.

• Trim the interfacing pieces to equal lengths.
5. Fuse and stitch the layers together.
• Set your steam iron on a wool setting and steam-baste the layers together.
• Cover the shoulder pad with a press cloth and fuse. Serge or zigzag the layers together along the edges

Diagram A: Serge or zigzag layers together.

(*Diagram A*).
6. Tack the shoulder pad in the armhole. (See Positioning Shoulder Pads below.)
7. Cover the shoulder pads with the extended facings (see page 92) and pin. Attach the facing to the sleeve seam allowance at intervals, using hand-sewn tacks or machine-sewn bar tacks.

Positioning Shoulder Pads

Shoulder pads add shape and stability to a jacket. It's important to get them in the right position.
1. Position the shoulder pad in the jacket.
• Place the shoulder pad on the wrong side of the garment shoulder seam.
• Match the center of the shoulder pad to the center of the sleeve cap.
• Extend the edge of the pad to the cut edge of the armhole.
2. Secure the shoulder pad to the jacket.
• Attach a tailor tack foot, and adjust the machine for a zigzag stitch.
• Lower the feed dogs, or set the machine as for sewing on buttons. (See your owner's manual.)

• Tack each end of the pad to the sleeve seam allowance by zigzagging over the tailor tack foot. Tack the center of the pad to the shoulder seam allowance (*Diagram B*).

Place tacks here.

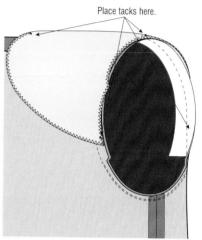

Diagram B: Tack shoulder pad to seam allowances.

pockets

Pockets can be functional or purely decorative. Shaping and stitching pockets don't have to be difficult or time-consuming. Even if your pattern doesn't include pockets, it's easy to add them using the techniques in this section.

Patch Pocket Basics

Patch pockets can run the gamut from a basic square to an elaborate shaped design. But no matter what the design, shaping these pockets involves a few basic steps.

Preparing the Pocket

1. Mark the pocket by making ¼" (6 mm) nips at the pocket hemline to indicate the fold line.

2. Mark the pocket position on the garment using a fabric marking pen or thread tacks (tailor tacks). To make thread tacks:

• Thread a needle, pulling thread ends to the same length and leaving them unknotted.

• Take a small handstitch through the pattern and fabric layers at the pocket placement dots.

• Cut the thread, leaving approximately 1" (2.5 cm) thread tails (Diagram A).

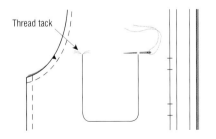

Diagram A: Mark pocket position using thread tacks.

• Repeat until you transfer all pocket placement positions to the fabric.

• Gently separate fabric from pattern at each thread tack. Clip the thread as close to the fabric as possible. Having short thread tails prevents the threads from pulling out of the fabric.

3. Interface the pocket.

• Cut a strip of interfacing the size of the pocket hem, including seam allowances.

• Fuse the interfacing to the wrong side of the pocket hem, following manufacturer's instructions (Diagram B).

Diagram B: Fuse interfacing to pocket hem.

Shaping a Square Pocket

1. Miter the corners.

• Measure and mark 1¼" (3.2 cm) from either side of one lower pocket corner. Repeat for the second lower pocket corner.

• Place a strip of Sewer's Fix-it Tape on the wrong side of the fabric between the two marks, extending the tape ends (Diagram C).

Diagram C: Place tape between marks.

• With right sides together, fold the corner to a point, aligning the marks and the tape.

• Stitch next to, but not through, the tape, forming the miter (Diagram D).

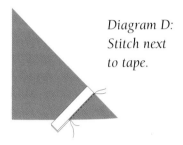

Diagram D: Stitch next to tape.

• Remove tape and trim the seam to ¼" or 6 mm (Diagram E).

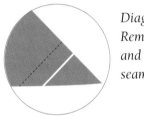

Diagram E: Remove tape and trim seam.

• Repeat for the second corner.

• Turn the mitered corners right side out (Diagram F).

Diagram F: Turn mitered corners right side out.

2. Press the pocket.

• Press the side seam allowances to the wrong side, using the straight edge of an Ezy-Hem Gauge as a pressing guide. Place the gauge on the wrong side of the fabric. Fold the seam allowance on one side of the pocket to the ⅝" (1.5 cm) mark on the gauge; press. Repeat for the other side of the pocket. The gauge acts as a buffer, eliminating seam show-through, and also serves as a measuring guide.

Note from Nancy

Because the Ezy-Hem Gauge is metal, it gets very hot when you press over it. Let it cool a few seconds before removing it from the pocket.

• Repeat this step on the lower edge of the pocket.
• Fold under the hem allowances at the nip markings, using the straight edge of the hem gauge as a guide (*Diagram A*). Prepressing the hem eliminates the need for stitching the side seams at the top of the pocket.

Diagram A: Use a hem gauge to press pocket sides and hem.

Shaping Pockets
with Rounded Corners
1. Press the side and lower seam allowances as for pockets with square corners, using an Ezy-Hem Gauge, but stopping prior to the corner curve.
2. Use a Pocket Curve Template to shape the corner.
• Place one of the template's corner curves on the wrong side of the fabric along the pocket seam line. Align the straight sections of the template with the prepressed side and lower press marks.
• Mold the corner seam allowance over the template.
• Attach the clip section of the template to hold the seam allowance in place (*photo below*). Press. If necessary, trim excess seam allowances.

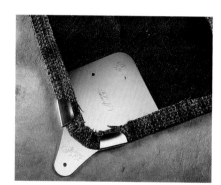

Clip a Pocket Curve Template in place to shape rounded pocket corners.

• Repeat on second pocket corner.
• Press the hem edge as detailed for pockets with square corners.

Shaping Pockets
with Designer Corners
1. Place the paper pattern on the right side of the pocket. Place a pin in the center of the pattern to anchor it.
2. Place the pocket wrong side up on an ironing board. Use a dry iron to fold and press one side seam allowance to the wrong side, using the pattern's stitching line as a guide.
3. Repeat, shaping remaining corners in sequence.
4. Press under the hem edge as detailed for pockets with square corners.

Positioning and Stitching Pockets
1. Place the pocket on the right side of the garment, matching pocket top corners to pocket position marks. Because stitching over pins sometimes causes uneven topstitching, use one of the following techniques to position the pocket.
• Use strips of Sewer's Fix-it Tape. Stitching perforates the tape, so you can easily remove it after you finish stitching.
• Use narrow strips of paper-backed fusible web. This is especially helpful with casual fabrics.
•• Cut a ¼" (6 mm) strip of paper-backed fusible web.
•• Position the web strips on the pocket seam allowances, just inside the pocket edge. Use a dry iron to press the strips in place. Peel off the paper backing (*Diagram B*).

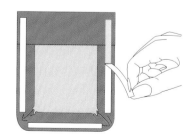

Diagram B: Use fusible web strips to position pockets.

2.   Stitch the pocket in place.

• Replace the conventional sewing machine presser foot with an edge joining foot or a blindhem foot. The edge joining foot has a center metal guide; butt the edge of the pocket against this guide and stitch. The blindhem foot is a standard accessory to many machines; place the edge of the pocket against the foot's adjustable bar and stitch.

• Adjust the machine stitch length to 0; bar-tack in place several stitches to reinforce the top edge of the pocket (*Diagram C*).

Diagram C: Bar-tack at upper corners.

• Stop with the needle down in the fabric. Return to normal stitch length and edgestitch close to the pocket edge, stopping at the other top edge of the pocket, with the needle down in the fabric.

• Adjust stitch length to 0; bar-tack.

• If desired, add a second row of stitching parallel to the first stitching, using one of the following methods.

•• Adjust the presser foot guide bar, positioning the second row of stitching $^1/_8$" to $^1/_4$" (3 mm to 6 mm) from the first row of stitching.

•• Or, change the needle to the left position and stitch again, guiding the edge of the pocket against the foot's guide or bar.

3.   If desired, reinforce the upper edge of the pocket as follows.

• Place marks $^1/_4$" (6 mm) from the corners on the top edge and $^1/_2$" (1.3 cm) from the corners along each side edge.

• Stitch from the $^1/_2$" (1.3 cm) mark to the $^1/_4$" (6 mm) mark at an angle; pivot.

• Take two stitches across the top edge of the pocket; pivot. Stitch around the pocket, repeating the reinforcement at the opposite top edge.

Working with Plaids

When you sew a garment using plaid fabric, consider either of the following ideas for adding patch pockets.

1.   Match the plaid on the pocket to the plaid on the garment.

• Cut out the garment section; use crossed pins to mark the position for the corners of the pockets.

• Before cutting out the pocket piece, place the pocket pattern on the cut-out garment section, matching corresponding marks (*Diagram D*).

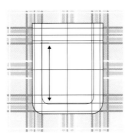

Diagram D: Line up pocket pattern with garment plaid.

• Use colored pencils to draw key plaid lines from the garment onto the pocket pattern.

• Place the pocket pattern on the fabric, aligning the colored lines on the pattern with the fabric design lines. Cut out the pocket.

2.   Eliminate the need for matching by using the pocket as an accent. Place the pocket pattern on a grain line different from that of the garment. If you cut the garment on the straight of grain, cut the pocket on the bias (*Diagram E*). If you cut the garment on the bias, cut the pocket on the straight of grain.

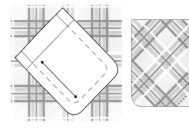

Diagram E: Cut plaid pockets on bias.

Flatter Pocket Flaps

Stitching pocket flaps the traditional way sometimes results in extra bulk at the outer edges. Here's a unique way of repositioning seams to eliminate that bulk.

1.   Cut interfacing for the flap.

• Fold the side seams of the flap pattern to the wrong side.

• Cut two layers of fusible interfacing from the folded pattern.

2.   Modify the flap pattern.

• Unfold the pattern side seams. Make a copy of the pocket flap pattern by tracing it or photocopying it.

• Machine-baste the two paper flap patterns together along each side seam.

• Mark a new vertical seam on the top flap, to the right of the center. Cut the top pattern along that line, but do not cut the lower pattern (*Diagram A*).

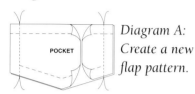

Diagram A: Create a new flap pattern.

• Open the pattern, unfolding it along the stitched seam lines.
• Tape a ⅝" (1.5 cm) seam allowance to each side of the new flap pattern (*Diagram B*).

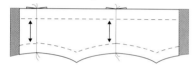

Diagram B: Add seam allowances to ends of new pattern.

3. Cut the pocket flaps from fabric, using the modified pattern.
4. Position and fuse the interfacing to the wrong side of the flap, matching the shape of the lower edge (*Diagram C*).

Diagram C: Fuse interfacing to flap.

5. Stitch the flap seams.
• Stitch the vertical seam, right sides together (*Diagram D*).

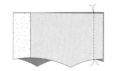

Diagram D: Stitch flap's vertical seam.

• Press the seam open.
• Refold the flap, aligning lower edges. Stitch the lower edge seam (*Diagram E*).

Diagram E: Refold flap; stitch lower edge.

• Grade the seam, and angle-cut the corners. Turn the flap right side out. Because the seam doesn't lie at the outer edge of the flap, there's less bulk.
6. Edgestitch the outer edge of the flap.
7. Stitch the flap to the garment.
• Invert the flap; position its stitching line along the marked flap position on the garment. Sew along the stitching line (*Diagram F*).

Diagram F: Invert flap; stitch.

• Fold the outer corners of the seam allowance to meet the first stitching line. Stitch a presser-foot width away from the first stitching (*Diagram G*).

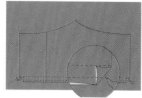

Diagram G: Fold outer corners in; stitch.

• Trim off any remaining seam allowance. If necessary, zigzag the edges.

Speedy Lined Patch Pockets

A lining provides greater shape and prevents a pocket from sagging. Keeping the lining from peeking out around the edges of the pocket has always been the most challenging part of stitching a lined patch pocket. Here are two techniques that slightly change the shape of the lining to keep it in place. The result is a smooth, professional looking pocket.

1. Interface the pocket.
• Fold under the hem allowance of the pocket pattern. Cut interfacing to this size, including seam allowances.

Note from Nancy

Traditionally, I've trimmed ½" (1.3 cm) from interfacing seam allowances because I felt this eliminated bulk. But, after taking a look at what's done in ready-to-wear, I take a different approach. I now interface to the cut edges, including seam allowances. Doing so doesn't seem to add much bulk, and it definitely saves time.

• Fuse the interfacing to the wrong side of the pocket.
2. Press under the hem allowance, using the Ezy-Hem Gauge.
3. Clean-finish the hem edge in either of the following ways.
• Zigzag or serge the edge, attaching a narrow ¼" (6 mm) strip of

fusible web to the wrong side of the hem allowance at the same time (*Diagram H*).

Diagram H: Zigzag or serge web to wrong side of hem allowance.

• Serge or zigzag the edge, right side up, threading the lower looper or bobbin with fusible thread such as ThreadFuse.

4.   Fold the hem to the outside of the pocket along the pressed edges, right sides together. Pin along the side seam.

5.   Cut a pocket lining.

• Cut the lining the size of the finished pocket, eliminating the pocket hem allowance (*Diagram I*).

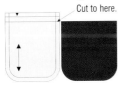
Cut to here.

Diagram I: Fold under top hem allowance of pattern to make pocket lining pattern.

• Trim ⅛" (3 mm) or less from the outer and lower edges of the lining, but not from the top edge. This makes the lining slightly smaller than the actual pocket, so it won't roll to the outside when you finish the pocket.

6.   Stitch the lining to the pocket.

• Match the cut edges of the lining

and pocket, right sides together. The edges meet perfectly on one side, but since the lining is slightly smaller than the pocket, you have to force the edges to meet on the second side.

• Stitch around the entire pocket with a ⅝" (1.5 cm) seam allowance, beginning at one folded edge and stitching to the second folded edge.

• Press the seam flat. Do not press the top hem edge; doing so would fuse the hem, and this edge must remain open for turning.

• Grade the seam. Use pinking shears to eliminate bulk quickly and accurately. Or grade the seam, making one edge narrower than the other.

7.   Turn the pocket right side out and press. Use a Bamboo Pointer & Creaser to shape the pocket edges. The fusible thread or fusible web seals the hem edge. Because the lining is slightly smaller than the outer pocket, the pocket seams will roll to the inside.

8.   Position the pocket on the garment and edgestitch.

All-in-One Side Pockets

Traditional side pocket applications require four seams, which may add bulk. By combining pattern pieces before you cut, you save time and eliminate much of that bulk.

1.   Make a duplicate of the pocket pattern piece out of tissue or waxed paper, transferring all markings. Be sure to mark the dots where the side seams should end at the top and bottom of the pocket. Using a photocopier is a quick and easy

Streamline your pants or skirts by making an all-in-one side pocket.

way to make a duplicate pattern.

2.   Place the original pocket pattern piece over the garment front pattern piece, aligning markings and stitching lines (*Diagram J*). Pin or tape the two pattern pieces together. Repeat on the garment back.

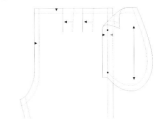

Diagram J: Modify pattern to eliminate pocket seam.

3. Cut out the garment, using the modified front and back patterns.

4. Transfer pattern markings.

5. Stitch and complete the pocket.

• Meet right sides of garment front and back. Stitch the side seam from the hem edge to the dot marking the lower edge of the pocket opening. Pivot and continue stitching around the pocket to the waistline edge.

• Stitch the side seam from the upper pocket opening to the waist-line (*Diagram A*). To reinforce this stitching, sew again over the first line of stitching.

Diagram A: Stitch garment pieces together.

• On the back garment section, clip the seam allowance to the pivot point. Press the seam open, press-ing the pocket toward the front (*Diagram B*).

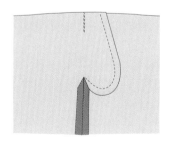

Diagram B: Clip and press seam.

Double Welt Pockets

A double welt pocket is the trade-mark of a tailored jacket. If you've avoided making these pockets because you felt they were too dif-ficult, here's an easy way to achieve a professional result.

1. Stitch the pocket window.

• Transfer the pocket placement markings to the right side of the jacket fabric.

• Trace a copy of the portion of the lining pattern that includes the welt opening. Position the traced copy over the lining, matching markings. This copy serves as a stabilizer and provides an accurate stitching guide (*Diagram C*).

Diagram C: Trace copy of welt opening.

• Cut out the pocket lining, and transfer markings. With right sides together, pin the lining to the garment, matching markings.

• Replace the conventional presser foot with an open toe foot. This foot provides greater visibility for stitch-ing, making it easier to stitch corners accurately.

• Adjust the machine for a short stitch, using a 1.5 setting (20 stitches per inch). Using a short stitch length secures the stitching and perforates the paper more thoroughly.

• Lower the sewing machine needle at the center of the stitching line on one side of the welt opening. Stitch around the opening, following the traced lines and pivoting at corners (*Diagram D*). Using the paper as a guide provides a precise stitching line, making the finished window accurate and precise.

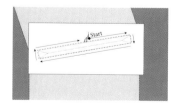

Diagram D: Stitch through photo-copy pattern.

2. Remove the paper. Clip through the center of the window, cutting to within ¼" (6 mm) of the corners (*Diagram E*). Then snip carefully into each corner. Optional: Restitch the opening for reinforcement after cutting, especially on loosely woven fabrics.

Diagram E: Clip window.

3. Press one side of the lining toward the center of the opening, over the seam allowance (*Diagram F*). Understitch the lengthwise edge and then repeat for the other lengthwise edge. These stitches won't show on the finished pocket, but they help keep the lining in place and provide a crisp edge when you complete the pocket.

Diagram F: Press one side of lining toward center.

4. Turn the pocket lining to the wrong side of the jacket and press, creating a window for the welt (*Diagram G*).

Diagram G: Turn lining to wrong side; press.

5. Prepare the welt.
• Cut two strips of garment fabric, each 2" (5 cm) wide and 2" (5 cm) longer than the pocket window.
• Place the two strips right sides together and machine-baste along the center of the strips (*Diagram H*).

Diagram H: Baste down center of welt.

• Refold the strips, exposing fabric right sides (*Diagram I*). Press.

Diagram I: Refold strip; press.

6. Position the welts under the window and fuse-baste in place.
• Place narrow (¼"-wide or 6 mm-wide) strips of paper-backed fusible web on the wrong side of the jacket, along the lengthwise edges of the window; press (*Diagram J*). Remove the paper backing from the strips.

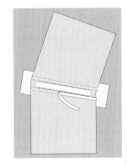

Diagram J: Fuse strips of web to window.

• Place the welt on a pressing surface. Position the jacket window, right side up, over the welt, centering the welt in the window (*Diagram K*). Cover with a press cloth and fuse.

Diagram K: Center welt in window.

7. Stitch the welts in place.
• Fold back the jacket front, exposing the original stitching for the top of the pocket window. Restitch along the original stitching line, or just a thread-width short of that stitching (*Diagram L*).

Diagram L: Expose original stitching; restitch.

• Repeat for the lower original stitching line and each short end.
8. Fold back the garment fabric. Zigzag the lengthwise cut edges of the welt to the lining (*Diagram M*). Don't include the garment in the stitching. Repeat for the remaining lengthwise cut edge.

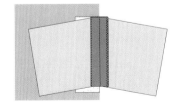

Diagram M: Zigzag welt to lining.

9. Complete the pocket following pattern instructions.

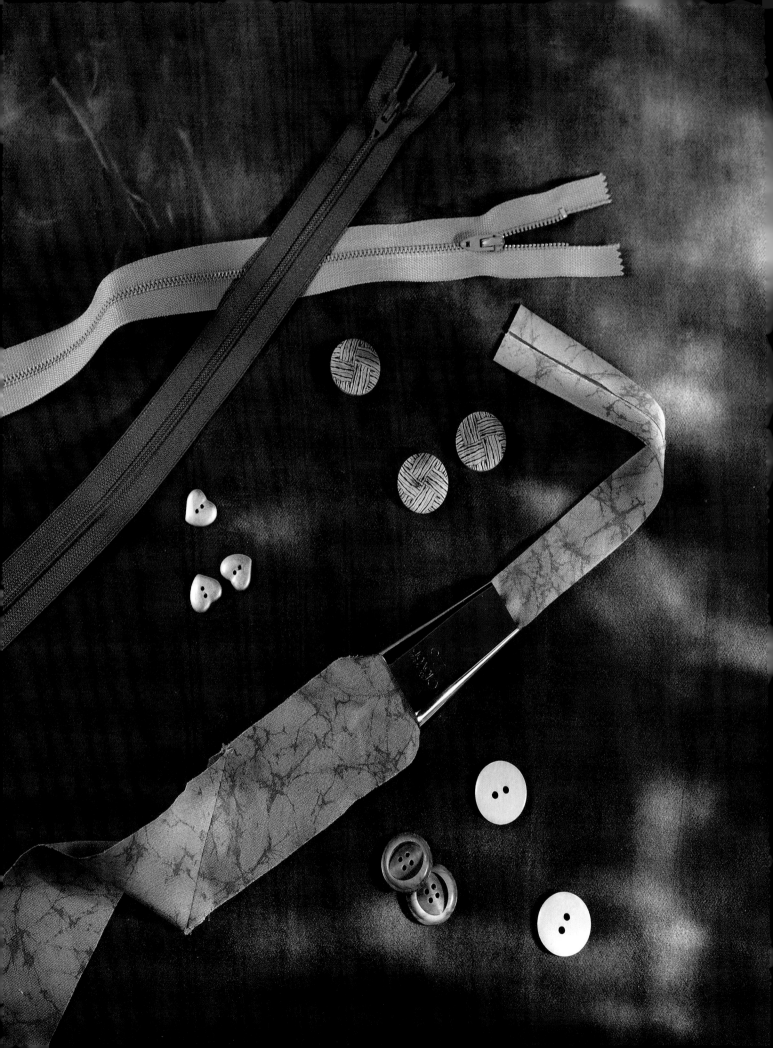

FINISHING

Done properly, your garment's finishing touches—hem, zipper, buttons and buttonholes—provide a final couture touch. But if you don't know the secrets to professional-quality finishing, these same touches may make your garment look homemade instead of handmade. • **I'll show you the quickest and best way** to center a zipper or give it a lapped finish, to sew on buttons and to make corded buttonholes. Piping, ribbing, scallops, and other special finishings not only dress up a project, but they can also give it a unique look. • **My finishing secrets** will give you better results and save you time.

Because many garments have zippers, almost every sewing machine comes with a zipper foot as a standard accessory. This specialized foot has only one toe, which allows you to stitch close to the zipper teeth.

There's no single right way to insert a zipper. The most common type of installation is called a lapped-insertion zipper, because a flap of fabric laps over the the zipper when it's closed (*Diagram A*). You can also sew a centered zipper, where fabric meets in the center over the zipper coils, or a mock hand-picked zipper that looks as if you sewed it in by hand. Pants often call for a fly-front zipper, which is a special kind of lapped-insertion zipper. For some outerwear, you may want to serge your zipper in place, a method that exposes the zipper.

Quick Two-Seam Lapped Zipper
If your previous experiences with inserting zippers were enough to make your blood boil, relax! Eliminate the hassle by using my updated technique. It requires only an increased seam allowance, two rows of machine stitching, and a little pressing.

1. Purchase the zipper at least 1" to 2" (2.5 cm to 5 cm) longer than needed. For example, if the pattern calls for a 7" (18 cm) zipper, buy one 9" (23 cm) long. The added length allows you to extend the zipper beyond the top of the garment during construction, ensuring even stitching in the zipper tab area.

2. Increase the zipper seam allowance.
• Add ³⁄₈" (1 cm) to the seam allowance in the zipper area (for a total of 1" or 2.5 cm) as you cut out the pattern (*Diagram B*). This wider seam allowance gives you more fabric to work with, so that you don't run out when stitching the lap of the zipper.

• Cut a ¼" (6 mm) clip marking at the stitching line at the top of the zipper opening on both the left and the right seam allowances. These markings are extremely important.

3. Stitch the seam below the zipper opening, stopping at the dot that marks the zipper opening and its wider seam allowance. Lock your stitches at the dot by sewing in place several times with the machine's stitch length set at 0.

4. Press the seam.
• Press the seam open below the zipper opening.
• On the garment's left side, fold and press under the entire 1" (2.5 cm) seam allowance in the zipper area. Use the clip marking and the lower end of the zipper opening to position the fold line.
• On the garment's right side, press under ⁷⁄₈" (2.2 cm) of the 1" (2.5 cm) seam allowance to create the zipper underlay (*Diagram C*). The finished zipper will lap left over right.

Diagram A: A lapped-insertion zipper is the most common type.

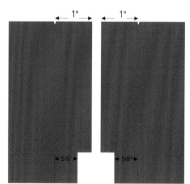

Diagram B: Add ⅜" to zipper-area seam allowance.

Diagram C: Fold seam allowances to create zipper overlap and underlay.

5. Insert the zipper.
• With right sides up, position the closed zipper under the zipper underlay, with the bottom of the zipper at the base of the zipper opening. Place the underlay fold next to the right side of the zipper teeth. Make certain the zipper tab

extends above the top of the garment. With short zippers, you shouldn't have to pin the zipper; merely finger-pin and stitch.

• Position your machine's zipper foot to the left of the needle. Stitch next to the fold, from the bottom to the top (*Diagram D*).

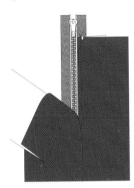

Diagram D: Stitch next to fold.

• Lap the garment's left side over the garment's right side, matching the nips. Tape the overlap in place.

Note from Nancy

Pins sometimes create dimples in the fabric, causing uneven stitching. I like to use strips of Sewer's Fix-it Tape about 4" (10 cm) apart to position the lap. This ½"-wide (1.3 cm-wide) tape keeps the edge perfectly flat and results in a more even topstitching. When you're finished, you can easily remove the tape, leaving no sticky residue.

6. Topstitch the lap.
• Align a strip of ½"-wide (1.3 cm-wide) Sewer's Fix-it Tape or transparent tape along the folded edge of the lapped seam allowance. This provides an accurate stitching guide. (*Diagram E*)

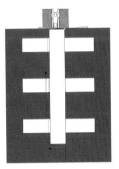

Diagram E: Use tape as a stitching guide.

• Slide the zipper foot to the right of the needle.
• Beginning at the base of the zipper, topstitch along the bottom edge of the tape and up the side.
• Remove the tape.
7. Complete the zipper insertion.
• Move the zipper pull down into the completed zipper placket. Satin-stitch or bar-tack over the ends of the zipper tape at the top of the zipper for reinforcement.
• Cut off the excess zipper tape (*Diagram F*).

Diagram F: Trim excess zipper tape.

Mistake-Proof Centered Zipper

Sundresses, jumpers, and garments with jewel necklines all have centered zipper openings at the back neckline.

Most sewing directions tell us to insert the zipper, apply the neckline facing, and then handstitch the facing edges in place over the zipper. However, with my timesaving sewing technique, you can complete the facing entirely by machine, minimizing bulk and eliminating all tedious hand sewing. Here's how to do it:
1. Modify and mark the pattern.
• Trim ¾" (2 cm) from the center back edge of the neckline facing (*Diagram G*).

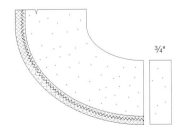

Diagram G: Trim ¾" from facing.

• Fuse the interfacing to the facing.
• Mark each side of the zipper opening on the garment back, ⅝" (1.3 cm) from the edge.
2. Insert the zipper.
• Stitch the garment seam from the bottom of the garment to the dot indicating the base of the zipper opening. Press the seam open.
• Fold under the ⅝" (1.3 cm) seam allowance from the base of the zipper opening to the neckline. Press.
• Open the zipper and unfold the seam allowance. With right sides together, align the zipper teeth with the crease in the fabric (Diagram A).

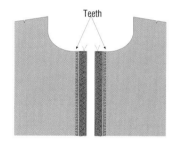

Diagram A: Align zipper teeth with fabric crease.

• Zigzag the zipper tape to each seam allowance.
3. Stitch the facing to the neckline.
• With right sides together, align the facing and garment at the center back opening. Stitch, using a ¼"-wide (6 mm-wide) seam allowance (Diagram B).

Diagram B: Stitch facing to garment back.

• Stitch the shoulder seams of the facing. Then stitch the shoulder seams of the garment.
• Align the shoulder seams of the garment and facing. Pin. The garment will wrap around the zipper at the center back opening (Diagram C).

Diagram C: Garment wraps around zipper.

• Stitch the neckline/facing seam.
• Grade the seam allowances and understitch. Turn right side out.
4. Topstitch the zipper in place.
• Close the zipper.
• Press the garment from the right side so that the fabric edges meet, covering the zipper teeth.
• Center a length of ½"-wide (1.3 cm-wide) transparent tape over the seam.
• Using the tape as a stitching guide, topstitch the zipper in place (Diagram D).

Diagram D: Stitch next to tape.

Two-Seam Fly-Front Zipper
This fly-front zipper application requires only two rows of stitching. You'll wonder why you ever let zippers create so much stress in your life.
1. For a standard 8" (20.5 cm) zipper opening, purchase a 9" (23 cm) zipper. Check the pattern to be sure the extension is 1½" (3.8 cm) from the center front and measures 9" (23 cm) long. If necessary, add width to the extension until it totals 1½" or 3.8 cm (Diagram E).

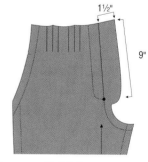

Diagram E: Make sure zipper extension is correct size.

2. Mark the zipper position on the front of the pants.
• Mark the center front of the fabric with a nip.

- On the wrong side, mark the zipper stopping point.
- Mark the front pattern pieces with R and L (right and left, as you would wear them) in the waist seam allowance, using a water-soluble marking pen.

3. Stitch the crotch.
- After you stitch the inseam and the side seam, turn one leg right side out, and insert it inside the other leg.
- Align the notches, seams, and raw edges; pin. Stitch crotch from waist to zipper stopping point.
- Restitch the crotch seam between the notches, and trim the seam to ³⁄₈" or 1 cm (Diagram F).

Diagram F: Restitch crotch seam between notches.

4. Press the zipper extension.
- On the left front, press under ³⁄₄" (2 cm) of the extension so that the fabric cut edge meets the nip.
- On the right front, press under the entire 1¹⁄₂" (3.8 cm) extension (Diagram G).

Diagram G: Press extensions.

5. Insert the left side of the zipper.
- Attach a zipper foot and adjust your sewing machine for a straightstitch.
- Place the zipper under the left front extension.
- Position the bottom zipper staple ¹⁄₄" (6 mm) below the zipper opening with the zipper length extending above the waistline.
- Pin the fabric fold of the left extension ¹⁄₈" (3 mm) from the zipper teeth. Stitch next to the fold (Diagram H).

Diagram H: Stitch next to fold.

6. Stitch the overlap section of the zipper.
- Lap the right front extension over the left, meeting center front nips. Pin or tape in place. See Note from Nancy on page 119 about Sewer's Fix-it Tape.
- Mark the stitching line using a water-soluble marking pen.
- Topstitch, starting at the bottom of the zipper opening, and curving the stitching line to approximately 1" (2.5 cm) from the fold (Diagram I).

Diagram I: Topstitch zipper.

Note from Nancy

To save time and ensure accuracy, I use a Fly-Front Zipper Guide when topstitching. The guide has tiny plastic "teeth" on its underside. Position the teeth in the seam line so that the distance from the seam line to the edge of the guide is 1" (2.5 cm). The teeth stabilize the template and hold the guide in place for accurate stitching.

- Remove the tape.
7. Open the zipper and bar-tack across the teeth close to the cut edge of the fabric. Trim the tape ¹⁄₄" (6 mm) above the bar tack (Diagram J).

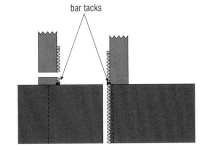

Diagram J: Trim zipper tape above bar tack.

Zippers for Knits

In the past, I found that zippers in knit garments tended to ripple and buckle. Now, with the help of fusible tricot interfacing and a paper-backed fusible web, installing a zipper in a knit garment is a simple 20-minute process. Here's how to do it:

1. Buy a nylon or polyester zipper that is 1" to 2" (2.5 cm to 5 cm) longer than the opening.

2. Cut two 1¼"-wide or 3.2 cm-wide strips of fusible tricot knit interfacing on the lengthwise grain, and fuse them to the wrong side of the zipper area. This lightweight interfacing stabilizes the zipper area, preventing the knit fabric from rippling as you insert the zipper.

3. Machine-baste the zipper opening closed. Press the seam open.

4. Cut two ½"-wide or 1.3 cm-wide strips of paper-backed fusible web. Fuse the strips to the wrong side of the seam allowances, and peel off the paper backing. Fuse the seam allowances to the wrong side by pressing the seam open.

5. Cut two more ½"-wide (1.3 cm-wide) strips of fusible web the length of the zipper. Fuse the strips to the right side of the zipper (Diagram A). Peel off the paper backing.

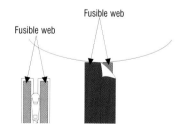

Diagram A: Fuse web to right side of zipper tape.

6. Center the zipper facedown over the seam, extending the extra zipper length above the neck edge (Diagram B). Press, fusing zipper in place.

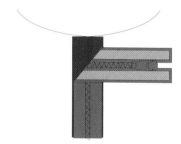

Diagram B: Extend extra zipper tape above neck edge.

7. Topstitch the zipper in place. (See page 120, Step 4.)

8. Remove the transparent tape and the basting stitches.

9. Open the zipper. Bar-tack across the top on each side of the zipper. Trim excess zipper length even with the seam allowance (Diagram C).

Diagram C: Bar-tack across zipper; trim excess length.

"Hand-Picked" Zipper

Sewing with a blindhem stitch rather than a straightstitch gives you the look of a hand-sewn zipper with the ease of machine sewing. This method works best with textured fabrics, such as woolens, tweeds, corduroy, or nubby-surfaced fabrics, because the stitches blend well with the fabrics.

1. Cut the skirt pattern with a 1" (2.5 cm) seam allowance at center back.

Note from Nancy

I prefer to cut out my skirt patterns with a 1" (2.5 cm) seam allowance at the center back. The extra width makes it easier to insert the lapped zipper, giving me a greater margin when topstitching the left side.

2. Stitch the center back seam with a 1" (2.5 cm) seam allowance. Use a standard stitch length from the hem to the dot and a basting stitch in the zipper area. Press the seam flat and then open.

3. Purchase a zipper at least 1" to 2" (2.5 cm to 5 cm) longer than needed.

4. Stitch the right zipper tape.

• Fold the garment fabric so that only the right seam allowance is exposed.

• With right sides together, open the zipper and place the right zipper tape on the right seam allowance, placing the zipper teeth next to the basted seam. Extend the zipper length above the seam.

• Use a zigzag stitch to machine-baste the right zipper tape to the right seam allowance (*Diagram D*).

Diagram D: Zigzag right zipper tape to right seam allowance.

• Attach the zipper foot.

• Set the machine for a straight-stitch with a medium stitch length.

• Close the zipper. Flip the zipper so that the right side faces up. Fold the seam allowance so that a ¼" (6 mm) fold forms next to the zipper teeth.

• Straightstitch within the fold area, approximately ⅛" (3 mm) from the zipper teeth (*Diagram E*).

Diagram E: Straightstitch next to zipper teeth.

5. Stitch the left zipper tape.

• Flip the left seam allowance over the zipper. Trim the seam allowance even with the zipper tape (*Diagram F*).

Diagram F: Trim left seam allowance even with zipper tape.

• Fold the left side of the skirt over the zipper.

• Fold back the skirt fabric along the left side of the zipper tape and the seam allowance until you expose ¼" (6 mm) of the seam allowance.

• Attach the blindhem foot and set your machine for a blindhem stitch.

• Starting at the bottom of the zipper, sew with a blindhem stitch, guiding the blindhem foot next to the garment fold. The straight stitches should fall in the seam allowances

and the zipper tape, and the zag of the blindhem stitch should catch the fold (*Diagram G*).

Diagram G: Stitch zipper to garment using blindhem stitch.

6. Turn the garment to the right side and remove the basting stitches.

7. Open zipper and bar-tack across top of teeth, close to fabric edge. Cut off tape above bar tack.

Invisible Zipper

Invisible zippers are a special type of zipper designed to look like a garment seam when closed.

1. Prepare the zipper opening and the facing.

• Do not stitch seam closed. The entire seam remains open during zipper insertion.

• Mark the ⅝" (1.5 cm) seam allowances for the zipper opening on the right side of both garment sections (*Diagram A*). This identifies where to position the zipper teeth during zipper application.

Diagram A: Mark seam allowances for zipper opening.

Note from Nancy

Most tape measures are ⅝" (1.5 cm) wide, so you can easily transfer that marking by simply placing the edge of a tape measure along the fabric's cut edge. Then mark along the opposite edge of the tape measure using a water-soluble marking pen or chalk.

• Trim ⅝" (1.5 cm) from the center back of both facings (*Diagram B*). A smaller facing later causes the garment to wrap around the zipper.

Diagram B: Trim ⅝" from center back of facing.

2.   Insert the invisible zipper.
• Press the zipper to flatten the zipper

coils. Doing so makes insertion easier. One word of caution: use a cool temperature setting. Since the coils are usually made of nylon or polyester, too much heat can damage them.
• Attach a zipper roller foot. The roller on this special foot allows it to glide over the fabric and zipper. The foot is also hinged to permit smooth stitching over bulky fabrics and crossed seams.
• Open the zipper. With right sides together, place zipper so one tape edge is even with edge of one back seam allowance, and zipper teeth are at marked seam line (*Diagram C*).

Diagram C: Place zipper with tape edge facing garment cut edge.

• Stitch next to zipper teeth from top to bottom. You will not be able to stitch completely to the bottom of the zipper; a short section remains unstitched.
• Close the zipper. Pin the unstitched side of the zipper to the remaining back seam allowance, right sides together. This ensures that the two sides of the garment will meet on the finished application. Open the zipper and stitch the second side of the zipper (*Diagram D*).

Diagram D: Stitch second side of zipper.

3.   Close the seam at the bottom of the zipper.
• Replace the roller foot with a conventional zipper foot.
• Reposition the zipper foot to the left of the needle.
• Meet garment seam edges below the zipper, right sides together. Stitch seam, overlapping a few stitches at the bottom of the zipper (*Diagram E*).

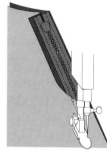

Diagram E: Stitch seam.

4.   Attach the facing.
• Stitch front facing to back facing at shoulder seams, right sides together.
• Pin facing to garment at center back, right sides together. Stitch a ¼" (6 mm) seam at each center back edge (*Diagram F*).

Diagram F: Stitch center back seams of facings.

- Meet facing to neckline, right sides together, matching shoulder seams. Pin. Since the facing is smaller than the garment, the garment wraps around the zipper, with the zipper teeth at the fold.
- Stitch the neckline seam. Grade and trim seam. Understitch seam allowances (*Diagram G*).

Diagram G: Stitch neckline seam.

- Turn facing to wrong side.

Serged Exposed Zippers

You can insert a zipper with a serger, although the zipper teeth will be exposed on the finished garment. Serged exposed zippers are especially attractive on sportswear and activewear. You may also like the look for pillows, garment bags, baby garments, and home furnishings.

1. Set up your serger for a 3/4-thread overlock stitch.
- Set stitch width at 5 mm to 6 mm.

Note from Nancy

It's important to use a 3/4-thread overlock stitch that incorporates both needle threads, since a zipper seam is subject to stress. If you have a 3-thread serger, reinforce the serged seam with a row of sewing machine straightstitching.

- Thread loopers and needles with all-purpose serger thread.

2. Position and stitch the zipper to one seam allowance.
- Purchase a zipper 4" (10 cm) longer than the zipper opening. This allows 2" (5 cm) to extend at each end so you don't have to serge over the zipper pull or stop.
- Open the zipper. Position it over the garment opening, right sides together, with tape extending 2" (5 cm) beyond each end. Place the edge of the zipper tape 1/8" (3 mm) from the cut edge of the fabric.
- Serge, guiding the left needle close to the zipper teeth. The serger foot will ride on top of the zipper teeth during stitching, and the serger knife will trim a portion of the zipper tape and seam allowance.

3. Position and stitch the remaining edge of the zipper tape to the other seam allowance.

Note from Nancy

Because the serger foot moves over the zipper teeth, the fabric tends to move around as you serge. To help you stitch an even seam, place a mark on the front of the serger presser foot at the position for the left needle stitching. Use this mark to guide the fabric during stitching.

- Close the zipper. Place the right side of the seam allowance over the right side of the unserged zipper tape, extending the seam allowance 1/8" (3 mm) beyond zipper (*Diagram H*).

Diagram H: Extend right seam allowance beyond zipper tape.

- Match upper and lower edges of zipper opening on both seam allowances. Use a glue stick or pin the zipper in place.
- Open the zipper and serge.

4. Working from the wrong side, press all seams away from the zipper.

5. Pull the zipper tab within the zipper opening. Bar-tack or satin-stitch across the ends of the zipper tape at the top and bottom to create new zipper stops (*Diagram I*).

Diagram I: Bar-tack across both ends of zipper tape.

Just about everything you sew has a hem—skirts, pants, sleeves, even home decor items, such as drapes and table linens. By using a few simple hints, you can turn this time-consuming chore into a simple sewing task.

• Prepress hems on each flat garment piece before stitching it to another piece. This is a great time-saving technique, especially when you're sewing children's sleeves, slack hems, or any circular area that's hard to press.

• Use an Ezy-Hem Gauge to provide an accurate measurement and to avoid leaving a hem impression on the right side of the fabric. Place the gauge on the wrong side of the fabric. Fold up the hem allowances over the gauge to the desired width. Press (*photo below*).

The Dritz Ezy-Hem Gauge simplifies measuring and pressing hems.

Easy Hems

Preparing a hem to stitch is a simple three-step process. Then you can choose any of several ways to attach the hem.

1. After stitching the side seams, press the hem at the seam areas. Grade the seam allowances within the hem area to reduce bulk (*Diagram A*).

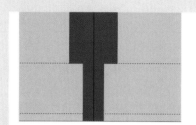

Diagram A: Grade seam allowance.

2. Finish the cut edge of the hem in one of these ways:
• Serge the cut edges.
• Edgestitch a presser foot width (approximately ¼" or 6 mm) away from the cut edge. Press under the hem edge, folding at the line of stitching.
3. Fold under the hem along the prepressed hemline and pin in place.
4. Attach the hem in one of the following ways:
   • Topstitch the hem in place.
   • Handstitch the hem in place. Use a single strand of thread and sew a blindhem stitch (see page 71). Cut the thread about 18" (45 cm) long; the thread will tangle and knot more easily if it's too long.

• Machine-stitch the hem using a blindhem stitch. Fold back the garment edge so that about ¼" (6 mm) of the hem edge shows (*Diagram B*). Stitch so that the straightstitch falls in the hem allowance and the zag just catches the garment at the fold (*Diagram C*).

Diagram B: Fold back garment edge so that ¼" of hem shows.

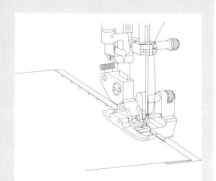

Diagram C: Straight part of stitch falls in hem allowance, and zag catches garment fold.

Fused Hems

Fusing is a fast and easy way to finish a hem. I like to use this technique on fun, casual clothes like shorts and skirts. Fusing works best on knits and lightweight wovens.

Note from Nancy

Try fusible web on a fabric scrap first to see if this is the hem finish you like.

Be careful when you fuse hems. Once the web melts, it's permanent. You have only one chance to get it right. If you think you may need to alter the hem length (which is often necessary in children's clothes), don't use this method.

To hem a garment using **unbacked fusible web** (such as Stitch Witchery):
1. Place a strip of fusible web ½" to ¾" (1.3 cm to 2 cm) wide along the wrong side of the hem edge.
2. Serge or zigzag the fusible web in place. Trim any web that extends past the edge (*Diagram D*).

3. Fold under the hem so that the entire hem is the same width (*Diagram E*).

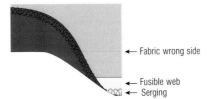

Diagram E: Fold up hem evenly.

4. Cover the hem with a damp press cloth. Press with a steam iron to fuse the hem to the garment.

To hem a garment using **paper-backed fusible web** (such as Wonder-Under):
1. Finish the raw edge by serging or zigzagging.
2. Cut strips of paper-backed fusible web ½" to ¾" (1.3 cm to 2 cm) wide.
3. Position the web side on the wrong side of the hem, placing the web ¼" (6 mm) above the hem edge; press.
4. Remove the paper backing (*Diagram F*).

5. Fold under the hem; fuse.

To hem a garment using **ThreadFuse and a serger** (especially useful for lightweight knits):
1. Thread the lower looper of the serger with ThreadFuse (a heat-activated fusible thread). Use all-purpose serger thread in the upper looper and needle(s).
2. With the right side of the fabric facing up, serge along the hem edge. The fusible thread will be on the underside of the hem (*Diagram G*).

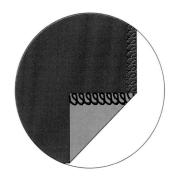

Diagram G: Fusible thread shows on underside of hem.

3. Turn up the hem to the desired length; fuse.

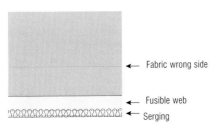

Diagram D: Serge or zigzag fusible web to hem edge.

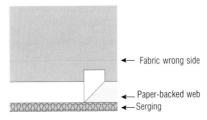

Diagram F: Press web to garment and remove paper backing.

Double-Needle Hems for Knits

A double-needle hem retains stretch or give in the crosswise grain, making it ideal for knit fabrics.

1. Press up the hem.
2. Replace your sewing machine needle with a double needle. (See page 149 for a needle chart.)
3. Working from the right side of the garment, stitch an even distance from the hem fold. When you finish, the right side of the garment will have two equidistant rows of stitching, and zigzag stitches will appear underneath, since the bobbin thread moves back and forth between the two needle threads (Diagram A).

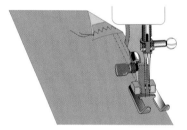

Diagram A: Double needles produce zigzag stitches on bottom.

4. Trim any hem allowance that extends beyond the stitching on the wrong side of the fabric.

Decorative Serged Hems

Use decorative threads in your serger's loopers to create a line of stitching at the hem of a garment (Photo A).

Since you expose the wrong side of the fabric, this technique isn't suitable for fabrics that look different on the right and wrong sides. Always test decorative serging techniques on fabric scraps first.

Photo A: Use decorative serging to hem a garment that has decoratively serged seams.

1. Set your serger for a medium-to-wide stitch width and a short stitch length. Use decorative thread in the upper looper. (See thread chart beginning on page 155.)
2. With the wrong side of the garment facing up, serge along the edge of the hem. You will be serging a single layer of fabric. To produce a more uniform stitch, allow the serger blades to trim the edge of the hem slightly.
3. Press the hem to the right side, exposing the decorative serging.
4. Using a conventional sewing machine, edgestitch along the serged needle line to complete the hem (Diagram B).

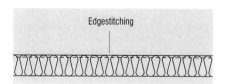

Diagram B: Edgestitch along serged needle line.

Hemming Pants

Mark your tape measure for fast pants measuring as follows:

1. Try on the pants (or a pair of pants that fits you), and place a pin at the desired length.
2. Lay the pants on the ironing board with the creases folded and the inseam and the side seam aligned.
3. Lift one leg and measure the inseam from the crotch to the pin. Mark this measurement on your tape measure (Photo B).

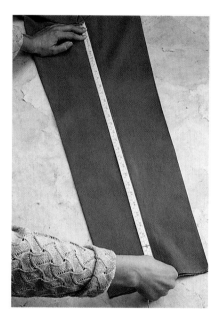

Photo B: Measure from crotch to pin.

Note from Nancy

By marking the inseam measurement on your tape measure, you'll never have to try on pants when hemming (unless you change your mind about length or your size changes). Use your marked tape measure every time.

Some sewing machines have built-in buttonholers, while others use special attachments. Check your owner's manual to see how your machine makes buttonholes.

Always sew a test buttonhole on a fabric scrap before working on your garment. Back the scrap with the interfacing and stabilizer you will use when sewing the garment.

> ### Note from Nancy
>
> *If the garment buttonholes follow the lengthwise grain, use that grain for your test buttonhole. If the buttonholes follow the crosswise grain, stitch the test buttonhole along that grain.*

Determining Buttonhole Length

Place the button on a flat surface. Start measuring at the bottom edge of the button, go across the top, and stop at the opposite bottom edge. Mark the starting and stopping points. This distance is how long the buttonhole should be (*Diagram A*).

Diagram A: Measure button.

Dependable Buttonhole Patterns

Machine buttonholes are one of the last construction details added to a garment. Sometimes the buttonhole placement markings you transferred to the fabric when you cut out the garment can disappear by the time

you need them. To avoid remarking the project, make a buttonhole pattern when you cut out the garment.

Make the buttonhole pattern out of a temporary stabilizer. In this innovative technique, the stabilizer serves two purposes: It supports the fabric and it marks buttonhole placement. Here's how to do it:

1. Cut a piece of temporary stabilizer 3" (7.5 cm) wide by the length of the buttonhole area.

> ### Note from Nancy
>
> *My favorite temporary stabilizer is Avalon Soluble Stabilizer. It's transparent and dissolves in water in seconds. You can also use an ordinary permanent marking pen on it.*

2. Place the stabilizer on the pattern, with one long edge on the fold line. Mark the stitching line at the neckline edge.

3. Trace the lines for the center front and the buttonhole placement (*Diagram B*).

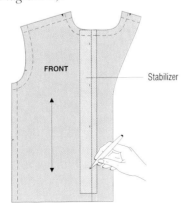

Diagram B: Mark buttonholes.

> ### Note from Nancy
>
> *Usually, horizontal buttonholes end ⅛" (3 cm) past the garment's center front or center back, and vertical buttonholes are positioned exactly on the center line.*

4. Stitch the buttonholes.

• Place the stabilizer over the buttonhole area, matching the buttonhole pattern to the fold line and neckline edges. Pin in place.

• Try on the garment. If no buttonhole falls at the center of your bustline, move the stabilizer strip up or down until it does. (A buttonhole placed at the bustline prevents the garment from gapping when you move your arms.) Repin the strip if necessary.

• Stitch the machine buttonholes over the markings on the stabilizer (*Diagram C*).

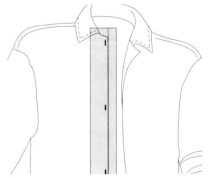

Diagram C: Stitch buttonholes over stabilizer.

5. After you complete all the buttonholes, tear away the stabilizer. (If small sections of the stabilizer remain, simply spritz with water to make them disappear.)

Stitching Corded Buttonholes

Adding cording underneath buttonhole stitching prevents the hole from stretching out of shape. Corded buttonholes are appropriate for jackets and coats, but because they add bulk, they are not usually suitable for dresses, blouses, and other lighter-weight garments.

1. Prepare to sew the buttonholes.

• Replace your machine's presser foot with a buttonhole foot.

• If your pattern does not call for interfacing between the buttonhole area and the facing, add a strip between the two fabric layers, cutting it slightly wider and longer than the buttonholes.

• Loop a piece of cording about three times the length of the buttonhole over the extra toe of your buttonhole foot (*Photo A*). Some feet have this toe in the front, while others are in the back. Place the cord's loop toward the center of the garment.

Photo A: Loop cording over extra toe of buttonhole foot.

Note from Nancy

I find that I get the best thread match for the cording by zigzagging over six strands of thread. You can also serge a chain using your garment thread, and then use the chain for cording.

2. Sew the buttonhole, stitching over the cording while holding the cording taut.

3. After you sew the buttonhole, pull the extra tails of the cording tight, and trim them next to the buttonhole (*Diagram A*).

Diagram A: Pull cording tight and trim close to buttonhole.

4. Flatten and press the buttonhole. The cording ends automatically withdraw and are hidden in the stitches.

5. Open the buttonhole using one of the following methods:

• Use a buttonhole cutter and block. (See Cutting Tools chart on page 140.)

• Use a seam ripper. To reduce the risk of cutting into the bar tacks at each end of the buttonhole, place a pin across each end (*Diagram B*).

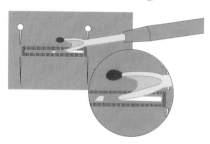

Diagram B: Place a pin across each end before cutting buttonhole open.

Hand-Sewn Buttons

Each button must have a shank for easy buttoning. A shank is a plastic or metal extension under the button. For buttons with holes and no shanks, here's how to add a thread shank:

1. Mark the button position directly under the buttonhole. Place the button over the mark.

2. Use a doubled, knotted thread. Hide the knot between the fabric and the button.

3. Put a small knitting needle, a round toothpick, or a large darning needle on top of the button between the button's holes.

Note from Nancy

Frances Mabry, who watches my public television show, "Sewing With Nancy," knots each strand separately when she sews with doubled thread. She's been surprised by how few tangles she has when using this method.

4. Sew five or six stitches through the holes, stitching over the needle or toothpick (*Diagram C*).

Diagram C: Stitch over a toothpick or a needle.

5. Bring the threaded needle up from the underside of the garment, between the button and the fabric (*Diagram D*). Remove the toothpick or needle on top of the button, and pull the button to the top of the threads.

Diagram D: Bring needle up between button and fabric.

6. Wind the needle thread tightly around the threads between the button and the fabric five or six times, forming a shank (*Diagram E*).

Diagram E: Wind needle thread around threads between button and fabric.

7. Bring the threaded needle back to the underside of the fabric. Tie knot close to the fabric.

Machine-Sewn Buttons

Use your sewing machine's fringe foot or tailor tack foot to sew on buttons. The foot's high center bar helps create the button's shank.

Note from Nancy

If you're sewing a button onto a garment that's likely to see a lot of stress—a child's garment or an athletic item, for example—use heavy-duty thread, such as embroidery floss or monofilament thread.

Here's how to machine-sew a button:
1. Use transparent tape to position your button on the garment. Place the tape on the button so that you won't stitch through it (*Diagram F*).

Diagram F: Tape button to fabric.

2. Set your machine in the left needle position for bar tacking (0 stitch length, wide zigzag). To check the correct width of the zigzag for your buttons, turn the wheel by hand to sew the first stitches (*Photo B, next column*).
3. Zigzag five or six times. Lock the stitches by setting your stitch width to 0 and stitching several times in the left needle position. Cut your thread, leaving 10" to 12" (25 cm to 30 cm) tails.

Photo B: Use tailor tack foot to stitch buttons.

4. Stitch the remaining buttons in the same manner and remove the transparent tape.
5. Form a thread shank.
• Pull each button up so that the excess thread forms a shank between the buttons and the fabric.
• Pull the long thread tails through the buttons and the fabric so that they meet at the shank.
• Thread the tails on a needle, and tightly wrap the tails around the shank a few times (*Diagram G*).

Diagram G: Pull long threads so they meet at shank; wrap threads around shank.

• Backstitch several times into the shank to fasten the thread tails. Seal the knot with a seam sealant, such as Fray Check.

Hems, zippers, and buttonholes are only three ways you can finish garments and home decor projects. You can also bind them, topstitch them, scallop them, or add piping, braid, ribbing, or other trims. These special finishes are often easier than you think.

Topstitching Tips

Topstitching adds a custom accent and enhances the stability of garment edges and other projects.

• Use double threads in both the needle and the bobbin to give a more balanced tension.

• Use a topstitching needle or a machine embroidery needle with an extra-large eye to accommodate the two threads. (See the needle chart on page 149.)

• Lengthen the stitch slightly to approximately eight stitches per inch, and adjust the needle and bobbin tensions.

• To stitch two perfectly parallel rows of topstitching, use a double needle.

Perfect Piping

Creating and inserting piping on fashions, home furnishings, and craft projects is easy.

1.   Make the piping.

• Cut bias strips 2" to 2½" (5 cm to 6.3 cm) wide by the needed length. Cut cording the same length as the bias strips.

• With wrong sides together, fold the strip lengthwise, sandwiching the cording inside the fold.

• Attach the cording foot. Position the cording so that it fits in the groove on the foot (*Diagram A*).

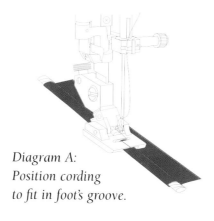

Diagram A:
Position cording
to fit in foot's groove.

• Adjust the needle position so that the stitching is close to the edge of the cording. Stitch.

Note from Nancy

If you can't adjust the needle position on your machine, attach a zipper foot and use it to stitch close to the cording.

• Mark ⅝" (1.5 cm) from the stitching line. Trim along this line so that the width of the piping seam allowance matches the width of the garment seam allowance (*Diagram B*).

Diagram B: Trim along marked line so that width of piping seam allowance equals width of garment seam allowance.

2.   Insert the piping into the seam.

• Sandwich the piping seam allowance between the two garment seam allowances, with right sides together and cut edges even.

• Place the cording in the groove of the cording foot.

• Change the needle position so that it lies close to the piping and aligns with the initial row of stitching (*Diagram C*). Measure to ensure that the needle will stitch ⅝" (1.5 cm) from the raw edge of the fabric.

• Stitch through all layers, catching piping in the seam.

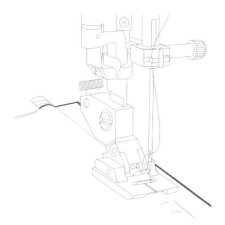

Diagram C: Change needle position so that it lies close to piping.

Note from Nancy

Traditionally, piping is applied in a two-step process: first, you sew the piping to one side of the seam, and then you stitch the seam. When you use a cording foot, it eliminates the first step, making this a one-step rather than a two-step process.

Adding Ribbing

One of the basics of sewing with knits is adding ribbing. Bands of ribbing provide an easy and attractive finish for neckline, waistline, and sleeve edges.

1. Cut the ribbing according to the guidelines below:
- For adult's garments, cut ribbing ⅔ the size of the neck opening.
- For children's garments, cut ribbing ¾ the size of the neck opening.

2. Seam the ribbing and fingerpress. Pressing with an iron can flatten and distort knit ribbing.

3. Fold the ribbing, wrong sides together, meeting cut edges.

4. Divide the ribbing into quarters, using the seam as one of the quarter points. Mark each point with a pin (Diagram D).

Diagram D: Divide ribbing into quarters.

5. Divide the neckline into quarters, using the center back and the center front for two of the points. Mark with pins (Diagram E).

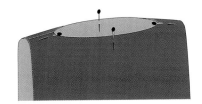

Diagram E: Divide neckline into quarters.

6. Pin the ribbing to the neckline, right sides together, matching quarter points (Diagram F). Place the ribbing seam at the center back.

Diagram F: Pin ribbing to neckline, right sides together.

7. Stitch the seam using a conventional sewing machine (below) or a serger.
- Using a conventional sewing machine, set machine for a narrow zigzag, using a 1.5 mm stitch length.
- Stitch with ribbing on top to help ease the longer garment section and allow better control.
- Stretch ribbing to fit the garment. Stretch only a small area at a time, rather than the entire neckline.
- Add a second row of zigzag stitching ¼" (6 mm) from the first row. Trim the seam to the second stitching (Diagram G).

Diagram G: Trim seam to second stitching.

8. Optional: Duplicate the look of expensive ready-to-wear by adding double-needle topstitching. Use a size 3.0 or 4.0 needle.
- Press seam toward garment using light pressure to avoid making an imprint. Or finger-press.
- If stitches skip, use a stretch double needle. These needles are specially designed to help prevent skipped stitches on knit fabrics.
- Working from the right side of the garment, topstitch below the neckline seam (Diagram H).

Diagram H: Topstitch below neckline seam.

Bias Binding

Rather than hemming a garment or adding facings, you might choose to add bias binding to the edges. By encasing the raw edges, you make a neat finish that can double as an attractive trim, especially if you choose a contrasting color for the binding.

You can purchase binding, but it's easy to make your own. Then you can stitch it to your project the traditional way, or use a fuse-and-stitch method.

1. Create the bias strips.
• Cut bias strips 2" (5 cm) wide.
• Join strips to make a binding as long as the edge you will bind.
•• Place one strip on the table, right side up.
•• Place a second strip perpendicular to the first, right sides together, and stitch a diagonal seam across the strips.
•• Trim seam allowances to 1/4" or 6 mm (*Diagram A*) and press seam allowances open.

Diagram A: Trim diagonal seam allowance.

•• Repeat until you create enough yardage to bind all your project edges.
2. Create 1"-wide (2.5 cm-wide) bias tape from the strips.
• Insert the bias strip, wrong side up, through the wide end of a Bias Tape Maker, advancing the strip with a pin. Fabric edges will fold to

the middle as they come out of the narrow end. Press edges as they come from the tape maker (*Photo A*).

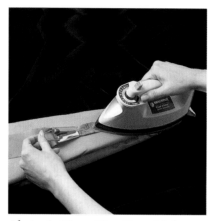

Photo A: Use a Bias Tape Maker to prepare binding.

• You can also use an iron to press the bias strip in half, with wrong sides together. Open the strip; press the cut edges to the center press mark; press again (*Diagram B*).

Diagram B: Press cut edges to center mark.

3. To make double-fold bias tape, meet the folded edges and press again.
4. Sew the binding to the project.
• Unfold one lengthwise edge of the tape. Meet that edge to the project edge, with right side of the tape next to wrong side of project.
• In curved areas, gently mold the tape to conform to the edge so that

it remains flat.
• Turn under 1/4" (6 mm) at the short edge of the bias tape; pin.
• Stitch the bias tape to the project, sewing just inside the first press mark (*Diagram C*).

Diagram C: Sew just inside first press mark.

• Where tape ends meet, lap the free end 1/4" (6 mm) over the stitched-down section. Cut off excess tape.
• From the right side, machine-stitch or handstitch the intersection of the tape ends together (*Diagram D*). Since the intersection is on the bias, it will be inconspicuous.

Diagram D: Stitch intersection of tape ends together.

• Wrap the tape to the right side of the project, meeting the tape's folded edge to the stitching line. Pin.

• Hand- or machine-edgestitch the tape in place, stitching from the right side (*Diagram E*).

Diagram E: Stitch tape in place.

Fuse-and-stitch binding.

The traditional method of applying binding (detailed in the previous section) requires two rows of stitching. You can eliminate one of these rows by using fusible thread, such as ThreadFuse. See the thread chart beginning on page 155 for a photo and description of fusible thread.

> ### Note from Nancy
>
> *Not all machines can handle the heavier weight of ThreadFuse in the bobbin. Always test on a fabric scrap first.*

1. Set up your sewing machine.
• Wind ThreadFuse onto the bobbin and place it in the bobbin case.
• Insert a size 100 needle or a topstitching needle. Thread the top of the machine with ThreadFuse. Because this thread is thicker than conventional sewing thread, you

Decorative finishes, such as piping on a jacket (left), can give garments a unique, couture look. Instructions for piping are on page 132.

must use a needle with a larger eye to accommodate it.
• Set the machine for a long basting stitch.
2. Stitch ¼" (6 mm) from the raw edges of the project wherever you will apply bias tape. The ThreadFuse will appear on both the wrong and the right sides of the fabric (*Diagram F*).
3. Wrap the bias tape around the edge of the project, covering the ThreadFuse stitching (*Diagram G*).
• Pin as needed.
• Where the tape ends overlap, turn under ¼" (6 mm) of the overlapping edge. Because the edges are on the diagonal, the bulk will be distributed.
4. Press, fusing the tape in place. ThreadFuse secures the binding, making it easy to stitch it in place.
5. Using conventional thread, edgestitch along the tape, stitching from the right side and catching

Diagram F: ThreadFuse appears on both sides of fabric.

Diagram G: Wrap bias tape around project, covering ThreadFuse.

both the inside and outside folded edges with a single line of stitching.

Symmetrical Scallops

Scallops make a stunning accent on a garment neckline, collar, or hemline, or on the bottom edge of a window covering. But getting those scallops evenly distributed and perfectly stitched can be a challenge.

You can use a tracing wheel or marking pen to transfer the scallop outline from the pattern to the fabric. However a photocopier gives you a more accurate and easy-to-follow stitching guide. Many grocery and convenience stores, post offices, and shopping malls have photocopy machines available for public use.

Try this photocopy technique the next time your pattern includes scallops:

1.   Photocopy the actual pattern piece containing the scallops.

• For patterns such as collars, where you need both a right and a left side, make one copy; then flip the pattern over to produce a mirror image for the second side.

• With large pieces, you may have to tape photocopied sections together to create the entire pattern piece.

2.   Meet garment sections (or garment and facing), right sides together. Pin or tape the photocopy to the fabric, aligning the edge of the paper pattern with the edge of the fabric (*Diagram A*). If you don't have access to a photocopier, transfer markings to fabric using a tracing wheel and tracing paper.

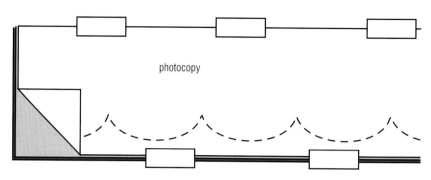

photocopy

Diagram A: Tape photocopy to fabric.

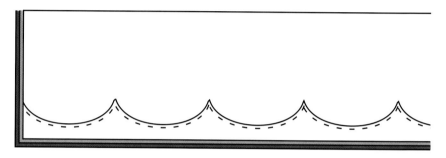

Diagram B: Stitch following outline.

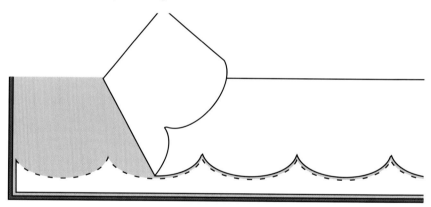

Diagram C: Remove paper in one piece along one side of scallop stitching.

3.   Adjust a conventional sewing machine for a short straightstitch. Use a setting of 1 to 1.5 (15 to 18 stitches per inch). The shorter stitch length makes it easier to obtain smooth curves.

4.   Stitch the scallops, following the outline on the photocopy (*Diagram B*). Stitching through this small section of paper won't harm the needle. (As with all sewing projects, it's best to insert a new needle before starting the project.)

5.   At the end of each scallop, stop with the needle in the "down" position and pivot to start the next scallop.

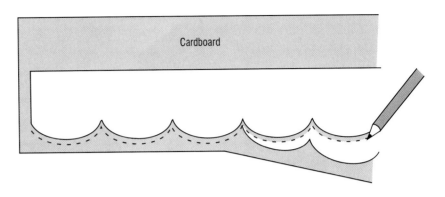

Diagram D: Cut out cardboard template, following traced outline.

6. After you have stitched all the scallops, remove the photocopy paper.
• The short stitch length perforates the paper, so you can easily tear it away.
• Try to remove the paper in one piece along one side of the scallop stitching (*Diagram C*). Use this paper to make a pressing template from lightweight cardboard as follows:
•• Trace the outline of several scallops on the cardboard. Cut out the template, following the traced outline (*Diagram D*).
•• If you transferred the scallop markings using tracing paper, transfer the scallop design to cardboard using a tracing wheel and tracing paper. Cut out the template.

7. Trim the scallops to reduce bulk.
• If you have curved embroidery scissors, this is an ideal time to use them, because the blade's contour is similar to that of the scallops.

• Cut to the point at the end of each scallop. Trim that area as closely as possible (*Diagram E*).

Diagram E: Trim end of each scallop as closely as possible.

8. Press the scallops.
• Press the scallops flat to set the stitches before turning them right side out.
• Turn the scallops right side out and insert the cardboard template. Press over the template, working from the wrong side and positioning the seam at the edge of the scallop template (*Diagram F*).

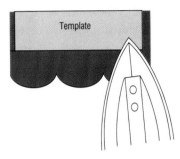

Diagram F: Press over template, working from wrong side.

• Pressing scallops takes time. Don't rush this step. Pressing accurately ensures that the completed scallops will be smooth and attractive.

CHARTS AND TABLES

When you're sewing, you may have a question that needs a quick answer. "What size needle should I use for this fabric?" "Isn't there a notion that would make this task easier?" "Can I use a Junior size pants pattern even if I normally wear a Misses'?" • **Charts and tables help you answer questions fast.** They provide comparative information in a compact format. For example, the table on page 149 gives the most common types of sewing machine needles and compares their uses and special features. • **You'll find a lot of useful information in these charts.** However, they aren't meant to be comprehensive. Manufacturers come out with new sewing notions almost daily, it seems, and types of interfacing, fabric, and other sewing essentials change almost as quickly. In some cases, I have listed brands that are common or popular, but you may find a similar product by another manufacturer in your local sewing or fabric store.

cutting TOOLS

Tool	Uses	Special Features
Appliqué scissors	Trimming close to edgestitching without cutting main fabric	Large bill lifts fabric to be trimmed, curved handles ensure comfortable hand position
Buttonhole cutter and block	Neat, professional-looking buttonholes	Cutter has hardwood handle with hardened steel blade, block comes in various shapes
Buttonhole scissors	Precise buttonhole cuts	Screw at handle holds scissors partially open, reservoir at base of blade safely holds fabric in front of buttonhole
Dressmaker shears	General sewing needs	Shears are 6" or longer, handles may be straight or bent
Pinking shears	Decorative, ravel-resistant finishes for seams and trim	Blades at least 6" long with saw-tooth edges, can be used to reduce bulk in curved seam allowances
Rotary cutter	Quilting, general sewing uses; can cut through several fabric layers at once	Works like pizza cutter, replaceable round blade retractable for safety, blades also available with wavy or pinked edges, use with rotary cutting mat and acrylic ruler
Rotary cutting mat	Protects work surfaces, provides guides for cutting straight edges; use with rotary cutters	Cutting side has measured grid, diagonal lines to help cut triangles; available in variety of sizes; store flat to prevent warping
Gingher® Sharpening Stone	Sharpens edges on sewing shears and scissors	Wipe blade clean after using

fabrics

Yardage Conversion

If the width of fabric you want to buy differs from the fabric width on the pattern envelope, use the conversion chart below to determine how much you should buy. Remember to buy extra fabric if you're enlarging the pattern or buying fabric with a large-scale or a one-way design.

Fabric Width	Yardage											
32"	$1\frac{7}{8}$	$2\frac{1}{4}$	$2\frac{1}{2}$	$2\frac{3}{4}$	$3\frac{1}{8}$	$3\frac{3}{8}$	$3\frac{3}{4}$	4	$4\frac{3}{8}$	$4\frac{5}{8}$	5	$5\frac{1}{4}$
35"-36"	$1\frac{3}{4}$	2	$2\frac{1}{4}$	$2\frac{1}{2}$	$2\frac{7}{8}$	$3\frac{1}{8}$	$3\frac{3}{8}$	$3\frac{3}{4}$	$4\frac{1}{4}$	$4\frac{1}{2}$	$4\frac{3}{4}$	5
39"	$1\frac{1}{2}$	$1\frac{3}{4}$	2	$2\frac{1}{4}$	$2\frac{1}{2}$	$2\frac{3}{4}$	3	$3\frac{1}{4}$	$3\frac{1}{2}$	$3\frac{3}{4}$	4	$4\frac{1}{4}$
41"	$1\frac{1}{2}$	$1\frac{3}{4}$	2	$2\frac{1}{4}$	$2\frac{1}{2}$	$2\frac{3}{4}$	$2\frac{7}{8}$	$3\frac{1}{8}$	$3\frac{3}{8}$	$3\frac{5}{8}$	$3\frac{7}{8}$	$4\frac{1}{8}$
44"-45"	$1\frac{3}{8}$	$1\frac{5}{8}$	$1\frac{3}{4}$	$2\frac{1}{8}$	$2\frac{1}{4}$	$2\frac{1}{2}$	$2\frac{3}{4}$	$2\frac{7}{8}$	$3\frac{1}{8}$	$3\frac{3}{8}$	$3\frac{5}{8}$	$3\frac{7}{8}$
50"	$1\frac{1}{4}$	$1\frac{1}{2}$	$1\frac{5}{8}$	$1\frac{3}{4}$	2	$2\frac{1}{4}$	$2\frac{3}{8}$	$2\frac{5}{8}$	$2\frac{3}{4}$	3	$3\frac{1}{4}$	$3\frac{3}{8}$
52"-54"	$1\frac{1}{8}$	$1\frac{3}{8}$	$1\frac{1}{2}$	$1\frac{3}{4}$	$1\frac{7}{8}$	2	$2\frac{1}{4}$	$2\frac{3}{8}$	$2\frac{5}{8}$	$2\frac{3}{4}$	$2\frac{7}{8}$	$3\frac{1}{8}$
58"-60"	1	$1\frac{1}{4}$	$1\frac{3}{8}$	$1\frac{5}{8}$	$1\frac{3}{4}$	$1\frac{7}{8}$	2	$2\frac{1}{4}$	$2\frac{3}{8}$	$2\frac{5}{8}$	$2\frac{3}{4}$	$2\frac{7}{8}$

Fabric Care

The end of a fabric bolt shows care instructions, but they're often given in numeric code. The following list explains what the code numbers mean:

1 Machine wash warm

2 Machine wash warm, line dry

3 Machine wash warm, tumble dry, remove promptly

4 Machine wash warm, delicate cycle, tumble dry low, use cool iron

5 Machine wash warm, do not dry-clean

6 Hand wash separately, use cool iron

7 Dry-clean only

8 Dry-clean, pile fabric method only

9 Wipe with damp cloth only

10 Machine wash warm, tumble dry or line dry

fabrics

Type	Weight	Needle Size	Thread	Special Concerns
Batiste	light	70	extra-fine	
Bouclé	medium	90, 100	all-purpose	
Broadcloth	medium	80	all-purpose	
Brocade	medium, heavy	80, 90	all-purpose	one-way shading
Calico	light	70	all-purpose	
Cambric	light	70	extra-fine	
Canvas	medium, heavy	100 denim, 110 denim	heavy-duty	
Challis	light	70	extra-fine	slippery
Chambray	medium	80	all-purpose	
Charmeuse	light	70	extra-fine	slippery
Chiffon	sheer	60	extra-fine	
Chino	medium	90	all-purpose	
Chintz	medium	90	all-purpose	
Coating	medium, heavy	100 denim, 110 denim	heavy-duty	
Corduroy	medium	90 universal, 100 denim	all-purpose	napped
Cotton/cotton blend	medium	90	all-purpose	
Cotton knit	light, medium	90	all-purpose	
Crepe	medium	90	all-purpose	
Crepe de chine	sheer	60	extra-fine	slippery
Crepon/crinkle cotton	light	70	extra-fine	
Denim	medium, heavy	90 universal, 100 denim	heavy-duty	
Double knit	medium	90, 100	all-purpose	one-way shading
Duck	medium, heavy	100 denim, 110 denim	heavy-duty	
Eyelet	light	70	extra-fine	
Faille	light	70	extra-fine	slippery
Fake fur	medium, heavy	90 universal, 90 stretch	all-purpose polyester	napped, slippery
Felt	medium	90, 100	all-purpose	
Flannel	medium, heavy	90, 100, 110	all-purpose	napped
Fleece	medium, heavy	100, 110	all-purpose	
Gabardine	medium	90, 100	all-purpose	one-way shading
Gauze	sheer	60	extra-fine	
Georgette	sheer	60	extra-fine	slippery
Gingham	medium	80	all-purpose	
Jersey	light, medium	90 stretch	extra-fine	
Lace	sheer	60	extra-fine	
Lamé	light, medium	80 metallic	all-purpose	slippery, metallic
Lawn	light	70	extra-fine	
Leather	medium, heavy	80 leather, 90 leather	all-purpose polyester	
Linen/linen type	light, medium	80, 90	all-purpose	
Metallic	medium	80 metallic	all-purpose polyester	test before pressing
Microfiber	medium	90 microtex	all-purpose polyester	

Type	Weight	Needle Size	Thread	Special Concerns
Mohair	medium	90, 100	all-purpose	
Moleskin	medium	90	all-purpose	napped
Muslin	light	80	all-purpose	
Net	sheer	60	extra-fine	
Organdy	light	70	extra-fine	
Organza	sheer	60	extra-fine	
Oxford cloth	light	70	all-purpose	
Plastic	medium	70 microtex	all-purpose polyester	
Polarfleece	medium	90, 100	all-purpose	napped
Poplin	medium	90 universal, 100 denim	all-purpose	
Quilted fabric	medium	90, 100	all-purpose	
Rayon	medium	90	all-purpose	slippery
Sailcloth	medium, heavy	100 denim, 110 denim	all-purpose	
Sateen/satin	medium	90	all-purpose	slippery
Seersucker	light	70	all-purpose	
Sequined fabric	medium	80 metallic, 90 metallic	all-purpose polyester	do not press
Shantung	medium	90	all-purpose	slippery, one-way shading
Shirting	light	70	all-purpose	
Silk/silk blend	light	60	extra-fine	slippery
Silk noile	light, medium	80	extra-fine	one-way shading
Spandex	light	75 stretch	lingerie/bobbin	stretch
Suede	medium, heavy	80 leather, 90 leather	all-purpose polyester	napped, one-way shading
Sweater knit	light, medium	90 stretch	lingerie/bobbin	stretch
Sweatshirt knit	medium	90	all-purpose	
Synthetic suede	medium	80 microtex	all-purpose polyester	napped, one-way shading
Taffeta	medium	80	all-purpose	slippery
Tencel®	*see Microfiber*			
Terry	light, medium	80 universal, 90 stretch	all-purpose	napped, may be stretchy
Tricot	light, medium	75 stretch, 90 stretch	lingerie/bobbin	slippery
Tulle	sheer	60	extra-fine	
Tweed	medium	90 universal, 100 denim	all-purpose	
Twill	medium	90 universal, 100 denim	all-purpose	
Ultrasuede®	*see Synthetic suede*			
Upholstery	medium, heavy	110	heavy-duty	
Velour	light, medium	90 universal, 90 stretch	all-purpose	napped, may be stretchy
Velvet/velveteen	medium	90	all-purpose	napped, slippery
Viscose	*see Rayon*			
Voile	sheer	60	extra-fine	
Wool/wool blend	medium, heavy	90, 100, 110	all-purpose	
Worsted	medium	90, 100	all-purpose	

*Needle sizes are for universal needles unless otherwise noted. See pages 26–27 for how to sew napped and slippery fabrics.

patterns AND FITTING

Pants Pattern Size Chart

Hip Measurement	Misses'/Petite	Juniors	Half Size	Women's
34"	6	5		
36"	8	7		
38"	10	9	10½	
40"	12	11	12½	
42"	14	13	14½	
44"	16	15	16½	38
46"	18		18½	40
48"	20		20½	42
50"+	22		22½	44

Front-Width Fitting Chart

Front Width	12"	12½"	13"	13½"	14"	14½"	15"	15½"	16"	16½"	17"	17½"	18"
Misses'/Petite	6	8	10	12	14	16	18	20	22				
Juniors	5	7	9	11	13	15							
Half Size			10½	12½	14½	16½	18½	20½	22½	24½			
Women's							38	40	42	44	46	48	50

FUSIBLE interfacing

You can use fusible interfacing for at least 90% of your sewing projects. Fusible interfacing has adhesive on one side only. Choose an interfacing that is lighter in weight than your fabric.

Types	Fabrics	Interfacing Brands*
Ultrasoft shaping of separates and dresses	Sheer, lightweight fabrics, such as batiste, chiffon, dimity, georgette, lawn, voile	Fusible Pellon® #906, Touch O'Gold™
Soft shaping of separates and dresses	Drapable light- to medium-weight fabrics, such as challis, jersey, single knits	Pellon® Easy Shaper #114ES, Fusible Pellon® #911FF, Soft 'N Silky™
Crisp shaping of separates and dresses	Medium-weight fabrics, such as broadcloth, chambray, cotton blends, gingham, lightweight denim, oxford cloth, poplin	Armo® ShirtShaper, Fusible Pellon® #931TD, Pellon® ShirTailor® #950F, Shape-up® Lightweight, Stacy® Shape
Allover shaping of coats, dresses, jackets, and suits	Medium-weight to heavyweight fabrics, such as corduroy, denim, flannel, linen, poplin, tweed, wool	Armo® Fusi-Form™ Lightweights, SuitMaker™, Pellon® Sof-Shape® #880F, SofBrush™, SofTouch™
Crisp shaping of coats, dresses, jackets, and suits	Medium-weight to heavyweight fabrics, such as gabardine, mohair, synthetic leather, synthetic suede	Armo® Form-Flex™ Nonwoven, Armo® Fusi-Form™ Suitweight, Pellon® Pel-Aire® #881, Whisper Weft™
Knits only	Cotton/blended knits, double knits, jersey, lightweight velour, single knits, sweatshirt fleece, terry	Knit fuze®, Pellon® Stretch-Ease #921, Quick Knit™, SofKnit®, Stacy® Easy-Knit® #130EK
Crafts	All fabrics	Pellon® Craft-Bond®

*New brands of interfacing are introduced often; check with your local sewing store staff.

Using Nonfusible Interfacing

Fusibles are not suited for the fabrics listed below. When using these fabrics, choose traditional nonfusible interfacing, such as Sewin' Sheer™ for lightweight fabrics and Stacy's® Woven Sew-In for light- to medium-weight fabrics.

- **Heavily textured fabrics**, such as tapestry and seersucker, because fusing flattens the surface of the fabric
- **Fabrics that are sensitive to heat, moisture, and pressure**, such as velvet and some silks, because fusing alters the surface
- **Fabrics treated with stain- or water-repellent finishes**, because the silicone treatment repels the moisture needed to bond fusibles

 **AND STABILIZERS**

Woven or nonwoven fusible web has adhesive on both sides, and it may have a paper covering on one side. You can also buy fusible thread and liquid fusible web, which act like heat-activated fabric glue.

Type of Web	Uses	Brands*
Paper-backed, no-sew fusible web	For crafts, home-decorating projects; use with light- to medium-weight fabrics; dense web gums needle if stitched through	HeatnBond® UltraHold, Pellon® Heavy Duty, Wonder-Under®
Paper-backed fusible web	For appliqués, hems; use with light-weight, medium-weight, or heavyweight fabrics; transfer designs onto paper backing, which acts as built-in pressing sheet; can sew through	Aleene's Original Fusible Web™, Aleene's Ultra Hold Fusible Web™, HeatnBond® Lite, Pellon® Wonder-Under® Fusing Web, Stitch Witchery® Plus with Grid
Fusible web	For appliqués, hems; use with light-weight, medium-weight, or heavyweight fabrics	Fine Fuse™, Stitch Witchery®
Liquid fusible web	For hems, appliqués, emblems, ribbons, and other trims; reposition ribbons, appliqués before you heat-set liquid fusible; bottle's applicator tip makes it easy to control amount and placement	Aleene's Liquid Fusible Web™, Liqui Fuse™ Liquid Fusible Web™
Fusible thread	For basting zippers, hems; heat and steam from iron cause thread to fuse fabrics together	Stitch n' Fuse®, ThreadFuse™

Stabilizers	Uses	Brands*
Iron-on stabilizer	Appliqué, machine embroidery; especially useful on stretchy, delicate fabrics; iron on, then tear away	Totally Stable
Liquid stabilizer	Appliqué, machine embroidery; apply to fabric and let dry; wash away after stitching	Perfect Sew
Tear-away stabilizer	Appliqué, machine embroidery	Pellon® Stitch-N-Tear®, Tear-Easy™
Water-soluble stabilizer	Machine embroidery on knit or woven fabrics; apply to right or wrong side of fabric; press away using a wet press cloth, or place project under water	Avalon® Soluble

*New brands of web and stabilizer are introduced often; check with your local sewing store staff.

marking TOOLS

Tool	Features
Chalk	Oil-free, several forms available • **Chalk Wheel** (*Bottom left*) contains loose chalk (white for dark fabrics or blue for light fabrics), transfers fine line of chalk to fabric • **Triangle Tailor's Chalk** (*Bottom right*) has chalk base in firm triangular form; comes in red, yellow, white, and blue • **Soapstone Fabric Marker** (*Top*) uses natural soapstone in an adjustable marker; marks are clearly visible, yet rub off easily when no longer needed; does not show up on light-colored fabrics; sharpens in pencil sharpener
Fabric marking pen	Pinpoint pen marks fine lines; useful for tracing small designs or marking complex patterns clearly; available in air- and water-soluble form; Wonder Marker is brand name of water-soluble fabric pen, which has blue ink that disappears with just a drop of water
Fabric marking pencil	Super-thin lead pencil specifically designed for fabric; contains less graphite than standard pencil; resists smearing, washes out beautifully
Gridded paper	Iron-on paper with ¼" grid; bonds permanently to other paper and temporarily to fabric; ideal for appliqué, stencilling
Hot Tape™	Adhesive-backed, heat-resistant gridded tape; useful for creating pleats or positioning appliqués; tape peels off easily without any residue; may be reused; sewing over tape gums up needle
Pattern Pals™	Pressure-sensitive symbols ideal for marking notches, dots, and circles on serger seams; eliminates need for nips
Pattern transfer material	Sawtoothed tracing wheel and tracing/transfer paper; paper is reusable, wax-free, and carbonless; marks erase, sponge off, or wash out; paper comes in variety of colors; The Fabric Pattern Transfer Kit™ includes transfer paper and special pen; use purple pen tip to trace design onto fabric, white tip to erase marks
Permanent fabric marking pen	Waterproof, permanent ink markers; work best on natural, untreated 100% cotton or cotton blends; use to personalize heirloom treasures, draw details on projects; not for marking patterns before sewing; Pigma Permanent Marker is one brand name

measuring TOOLS

Tool	Uses	Special Features
Curved ruler	Marking French curves; altering hiplines, princess seams, and other shaped seams	Most have straight and curved edges, brand name: Fashion Ruler™
Hem gauge	Measuring and marking straight and curved hems, and other turned edges	Usually made from metal, brand name: Ezy-Hem® Gauge
Quilting ruler • 1" x 6" • 1" x 12½" • 3" x 18" • Square • Half-square	Cutting precise pieces for quilting, patchwork; also useful in other sewing projects • Pocket-sized • Convenient size for quick measuring • Useful for patchwork and large projects • Useful for squaring up quilt blocks • Useful for cutting half-square triangles up to 8"	Made from heavy-duty, clear acrylic that rotary cutter blades won't nick; available in various sizes and shapes; larger sizes marked to help cut accurate 30°, 45°, and 60° angles
Sewing gauge	Marking hems, tucks, pleats, buttons, and buttonhole placements	6" long with a double-pointed slide, many marked in centimeters and inches
Tape measure	Taking body measurements; also useful for quilting, home decorating projects	Usually 60" (152 cm) long; also available in longer lengths, and with large numbers for easy viewing
Yardstick compass	Drawing circles for making tablecloths, quilts, and shoulder pads	Aluminum holders attached to a yardstick; one holder has a sharp metal point, the other a lead pencil point

Hem gauge

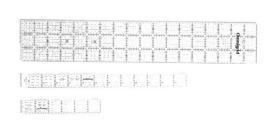

Quilting rulers

Needles	Size	Descriptions	Uses
Denim/Sharp	90, 100, 110	Very sharp point to ease penetration of dense fabrics	Denim, heavy corduroy, dense wool, canvas, heavy poplin or twill
Leather	80, 90	Wedge shape, knife-edge cutting point; not suited for synthetic suede or leather because slit made by needle eventually tears	Real leather or suede, not suitable for synthetic leather or suede
Machine Embroidery	75, 90	Slightly rounded point, long eye, and deep front groove; for use with decorative threads; protects delicate embroidery threads; avoids fraying and breaking	Knits and wovens
Metafil	80	Fine shaft, sharp point, and large, elongated eye; specialized scarf eliminates skipped stitches	Sewing with metallic and other decorative threads
Metallica	80	Large eye for easy threading and to accommodate heavier threads, large groove prevents shredding of threads	Sewing with metallic and other delicate threads
Microtex Sharps	60, 70, 80, 90	Slim, sharp point; very thin shaft for penetrating dense fabric surfaces	Microfiber fabrics such as Ultrasuede, heirloom sewing
Self-threading	90	Slit in side of eye for threading ease, weaker than conventional needles	Simplifies needle threading
Spring Denim/Sharp	100	Sharp point for penetrating dense fabrics, attached spring allows free-form sewing	Free-motion embroidery
Spring Machine Embroidery	75, 90	Same features as machine embroidery needle with an attached spring	Free-motion embroidery using decorative threads
Spring Machine Quilting	75, 90	Same features as machine quilting needle with an attached spring	Free-form quilting
Stretch	75, 90	Medium ballpoint; long, flat shank lets needle work close to bobbin; prevents skipped stitches	Size 75 for sewing lightweight knits, such as tricot, interlock, silk jersey, lycra, and Ultrasuede; size 90 for sewing lycra, Ultrasuede, and synthetic furs with knit backings
Topstitching	80, 90, 100	Extra-large eye, large groove accommodates topstitching thread	Sewing with heavier thread, embroidery with delicate and metallic threads
Universal	60, 70, 80, 90, 100, 110	Slightly rounded point, long needle scarf; all-purpose needle for sewing wovens, knits	Size 60 for silks; size 70 for lightweight fabrics; size 80 for medium-weight fabrics, size 90 for medium-weight to heavy fabrics, size 100 for heavy fabrics; size 110 for upholstery fabrics
Wing	100, 120	Wide, wing-shaped blades on each side create holes in fabric that look like entredeux trim	Hemstitch effect for heirloom sewing; best on natural fabrics, such as cotton, linen, silk, organdy
Double	1.6 mm/80 2.0 mm/80 3.0 mm/90 4.0 mm/90 6.0 mm/100 8.0 mm/100	Two universal needles on a crossbar; slightly rounded points, and large scarves	1.6 mm/80 and 2.0 mm/80 for pintucks, delicate heirloom sewing 3.0 mm/90 for hems, pintucks 4.0 mm/90 for decorative hems, surface embellishment 6.0 mm/100 for surface embellishment 8.0 mm/100 for adding texture to fabric
Double Machine Embroidery	2.0 mm/75 3.0 mm/75	Two machine embroidery needles on a crossbar, protects embroidery threads from fraying and breaking	Surface embellishment made with decorative threads
Double Metafil	3.0 mm/80	Two Metafil needles on a crossbar	Double stitching, embellishing with metallic threads
Double Wing	100	One wing needle and one universal needle on a crossbar	Special hemstitch effects and heirloom sewing on natural fabrics, such as cotton, linen, silk, organdy
Double Stretch	2.5 mm/75 4.0 mm/75	Two stretch needles on a crossbar, ballpoint prevents skipped stitches on knits	Pintucking, embroidery on knits, silk jersey, lycra, Ultrasuede
Triple	3.0 mm/80	Three universal needles on a single shaft	Decorative stitching

P R E S S E R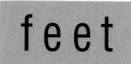

The presser feet illustrated in this chart may not look exactly like the feet in your accessory box, because each manufacturer has a different style. We've provided illustrations of generic presser feet and photographs of some of the specialty feet. To identify your presser feet, check your owner's manual, or compare the features listed in the chart with your presser feet.

Foot	Uses	Special Features
Conventional foot; also called a **general purpose** or **zigzag foot**	Everyday sewing	Has wide opening proportionate to width of machine's zigzag stitch (from 4 mm to 9 mm or ¹/₈" to ¹/₄", depending on sewing machine)
Blindhem foot	Hemming, applying patch pockets and appliqués, straight edgestitching	Adjustable guide moves closer to or farther from left side of foot to accommodate fabrics of various weights and textures
Buttonhole foot	Sewing identical buttonholes	Foot moves forward and backward in sliding tray attached to machine, markings along one or both sides of foot indicate buttonhole length
Cording foot	Making piping, couching cords and trim to fabric	Top of foot has wide opening for zigzag stitch; large groove on underside allows trim to lie flat, feed evenly under foot
Darning foot; the **Big Foot** is a large darning foot	Free-motion embroidery	Spring holds transparent foot against fabric
Felling foot	Making flat-felled seams, sewing ribbon to fabric using a double needle	Has opening or groove through which to guide fabric that's turned under as it passes beneath the foot, or to guide ribbon under the foot
Little Foot™	Accurate piecing for quilts	Transparent foot with red laser markings ¹/₄" (6 mm) and ¹/₈" (3 mm) from center needle position, as well as ¹/₄" (6 mm) in front of and behind needle; these serve as accurate reference points for starting, stopping, and pivoting when stitching ¹/₄" seam allowances

Foot	Uses	Special Features
 Multicord foot	Couching decorative threads onto fabric	Holes in front of foot guide up to five or more decorative threads under foot, optional **multiple cording guide** keeps threads aligned as they feed through machine
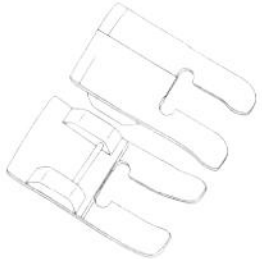 Open toe or embroidery foot	Machine embroidery and satin stitching	Toe area may be completely open, or its center may be clear plastic; underside has a hollowed or grooved section to permit dense stitching
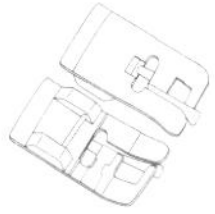 Overcast-guide foot	Overcasting edges of fabric that may curl or pucker with other finishes	Metal bar in center of foot's zigzag opening holds fabric flat while zigzag forms on edge of fabric
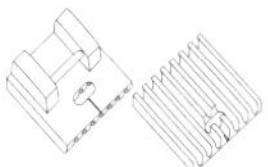 Pintuck foot	Stitching parallel rows of pintucks	A series of five to nine grooves on underside provide channels or guides for previous rows of pintucking
 Sequins 'N Ribbon™ foot	Stitching sequins, ribbon, and narrow elastic to fabric	Adjustable guide helps position trim precisely in front of needle for effortless stitching
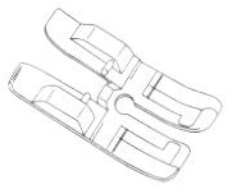 Straightstitch or jean foot	Stitching slippery fabric	Tiny round opening minimizes puckering, use it with throat plate that has a compatible round opening
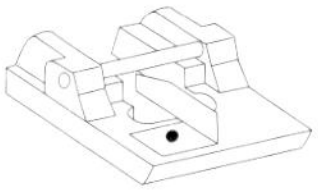 Tailor tack foot	Sewing on buttons and attaching shoulder pads	Vertical raised bar runs down center of foot; machine stitches over bar, creating loops
 Serger: Conventional foot	General serging	Usually has stitch finger, although some manufacturers put stitch finger on throat plate
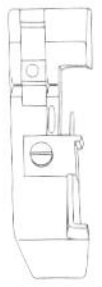 Serger: Specialty feet	Performing same functions as sewing machine feet	Commonly available feet include beading foot, blindhem foot, cording or piping foot, elastic foot, ribbon foot, rolled-edge foot (*shown at left*) and shirring or gathering foot

notions

Notion	Uses	Special Features
Bamboo Pointer & Creaser	Turn collars, cuffs, lapels, appliqués; temporarily press seams	One end pointed, other curved and beveled
Basting tape	"Pin" slippery, hard-to-pin fabrics; zipper stitching guide	$1/4$" wide
Beeswax	Strengthen thread; reduce tangles for hand-sewing, quilting, candlewicking	Comes in easy-application holder
Bias Tape Maker	Make uniform-width single-fold bias tape from fabric strips	Metal, 6 mm to 50 mm wide
Bodkin	Draw lace, ribbon, elastic through casings; weaving	Tweezerlike, with special teeth to grip trim or fabric
Clapper	Press sharp creases; flatten collars, lapels, pleats, facings, and other bulky details	Hardwood, some include point presser to press sharp points
Cone thread holder	Hold cone thread for use in sewing machine	Sits adjacent to sewing machine
Dressmaker's ham	Press small, curved areas	Sawdust or molded filling; cotton cover on one side, wool blend on other
Elastic glide	Draw elastic, ribbon, and other trims through casings	Various sizes available
Fly-Front Zipper Guide	Stitch curved zipper seams	Plastic teeth fit into seam, stabilizing tool for accurate topstitching
Hamholder™	Hold dressmaker's ham to free both hands for pressing	Holds ham upright, flat, or tilted at any angle
Jiffy Waistband & Ban-Rol®	Interface waistbands	Prevents waistband rollover, nonfusible
Little Wooden Iron	Temporary pressing, open seams	Hardwood, $5^{1}/4$" (13 cm) long, right- or left-handed versions
Magnetic Seam Guide	Stitch uniform seam widths	Adheres to metal throat plate, not recommended for computerized machines
Needleboard	Press napped fabrics, dimensional embellishments, such as silk-ribbon embroidery	Synthetic fabric covered with needlelike projections, brand name: Velvaboard®
Needle inserter	Insert needles into sewing machine and serger	Brush on opposite end cleans lint from machines, two-needle version available for sergers
Pattern weights	Hold patterns in place for cutting and marking	Assorted sizes and shapes, brand names: Weight Mates®, Shape Weights™
Pocket Curve Template	Shape pockets	Metal tool with four different corner shapes, clip holds fabric in place while pressing
Press cloth	Protect fabric surface, iron soleplate while pressing, fusing	Special types available for fusing, appliqué, setting creases and more; brand name: Steam 'n Shape™

Notion	Uses	Special Features
Seam ripper	Remove stitches	Has two prongs; one sharp to cut threads, the other ballpoint to protect fabric
Seam roll	Press seams without edge imprints	Cotton cover on one side, wool blend on other
Seam sealant	Reinforce and lock threads to prevent fraying of seams; use on buttonholes, ends of serged seams	Clear-drying liquid, brand names: No-Fray, Fray Check™
Seams Great®	Finish seams, facings	Bias-cut nylon, naturally curves over raw edges
Serger looper & needle threader	Thread serger loopers	Fine wire loop at one end, handle at other
Serger seam ripper	Remove serged seams	Slides under stitches, curved shape protects fabric from accidental cuts
Serger tweezers	Thread needles, loopers; insert needles	6" bent tweezers, locks when in use
Sewer's Fix-it Tape	Repair patterns, miter corners; zipper stitching guide	1/2" wide
Sleeve board	Press sleeves	Free-arm pressing surface, brand name: June Tailor Deluxe Sleeve Board
Stiletto	Ease fabric, lace, ribbon, seam allowances under presser foot	Awl-like tool
Tailor® Board	Press sleeves, sharp points and corners, seams, collars, lapels	Wooden surfaces, may be padded
Thread Pallette	Thread blending for serger or sewing machine	Holds up to 5 spools for serging, 3 for sewing; use with cone thread stand on sewing machine
Trolley Needle™ Thread Controller	Ease seams, ruffles, ribbon, other trim under presser foot	Thimblelike device slips over index finger
Tube turners • Collar Point & Tube Turner • Fasturn® • Narrow Loop Turner	Turn fabric tubes right side out • Also turn collar points, pocket flaps, other details • Also insert cording	Comes in various styles (see below) • Scissorlike device • Comes in variety of sizes • Latch holds fabric securely

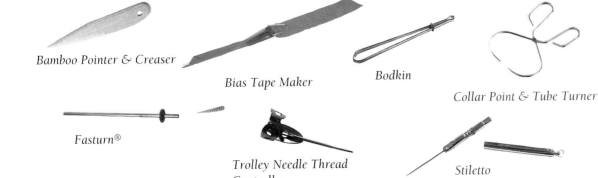

Bamboo Pointer & Creaser

Bias Tape Maker

Bodkin

Collar Point & Tube Turner

Little Wooden Iron

Fasturn®

Trolley Needle Thread Controller

Stiletto

Needles	Uses	Special Features
Ballpoint needles	Sewing knits	Rounded points push between knit yarns instead of piercing them
Betweens	Quilting	Sharp points, short length
Crewel needles	Decorative handwork such as embroidery	Long eyes handle several strands of floss or thread
Double-eyed needles	Weaving threads or trim underneath stitches	Blunt tips with eyes on each end
Sharps	General-purpose sewing	Round eyes, sharp points, medium length
Tapestry needles	Crafts such as needlepoint, use as bodkin	Blunt tips, large eyes, large shaft

Pins	Uses	Special Features
Appliqué	Pinning small pieces, tight corners	Short, thin shaft; flat head
Flower head	General-purpose sewing	Extra long; large, flat, colored heads make them easy to find in knits and textured fabrics
General-purpose or quilting	Pinning heavier fabrics and multiple layers	Medium length, flat head
Glass or plastic head	General-purpose sewing	Medium length; round, colored head
Silk or dressmaker's	General dressmaking	Flat head; medium length, diameter
T-pins	Upholstery craft projects, pinning loose knits	Long, T-shaped head

thread

Choose thread the same color or one shade darker than your fashion fabric. Thread appears lighter when sewn than it does on the spool. Match thread to the predominant or background color when working with prints, tweeds, or plaids.

If your stitches are not smooth and uniform, check the sewing machine needle for damage, size, and type. The needle should match the thread type, fabric, and sewing technique. The chart that follows includes descriptions of different thread types, their uses, fiber content, and size. Under the size column, the first number (Wt.) indicates the weight of the thread, and the second number (Ply) indicates the number of plies or strands used to make the thread. The larger the weight number, the finer the thread.

Always use three-ply thread for general-purpose sewing. Two-ply thread works well on sergers because serger seams use three or more threads, which strengthen the seams. I do not recommend using serger thread on your sewing machine.

Thread Type	Description	Uses	Fiber Content	Wt./Ply
All-purpose • Cotton-wrapped polyester core	Polyester core wrapped with fine cotton; less static than 100% polyester, easy to sew with; withstands high temperatures; can rot or mildew; more durable than 100% cotton—more stretch, strength	General sewing for most fabrics; avoid on leather, fur, suede, rainwear, and very lightweight fabrics	Cotton and polyester	50/3
• Long-staple polyester	High-quality polyester thread made with long fibers; stronger and more durable than cotton, and more resistant to abrasion and chemicals; may pucker seams and skip stitches in lightweight fabrics	General sewing for most fabrics, including leather, suede, and fur; avoid using on silk and lightweight fabrics	Polyester	50/3
Bobbinfil	Lightweight thread designed specifically for use in bobbins	Machine embroidery, decorative stitching	100% polyester	70/none
Buttonhole Twist	Thick, heavy thread; sometimes called topstitching thread; less lustrous than silk	Embellishment, topstitching	Polyester or polyester core	40/3

Thread Type		Description	Uses	Fiber Content	Wt./Ply
	Cotton	Lightweight thread, double mercerized for sheen and softness	Heirloom sewing, including smocking and embroidery	100% cotton	80/2
	Decorative and embellishment threads and yarns	Variety of threads, usually made from cotton, wool, silk, linen, acrylic, or silk-and-wool blend; dry-clean or prewash; some fibers may bleed	Surface embellishment, such as couching	Varies	Varies
	Embroidery • Cotton	Soft matte finish for a natural appearance	Embroidery, lace-making, quilting	100% cotton	30/2
	• Rayon	Brilliant, colorfast thread; available in solid and variegated colors	Decorative stitching, topstitching	100% viscose rayon	40/2, 30/2
	Fusible	Adhesive coating on thread melts when pressed with warm iron	Basting, substitute for narrow strips of fusible web	Twisted polyester thread containing heat-activated fusible nylon filament	85/3
	Jeans Stitch	Colorfast, durable thread	Topstitching, decorative stitching	Spun polyester	30/3
	Lingerie/Bobbin	Extra-fine nylon thread, good stretch, black or white only	Bobbin thread for decorative stitching, machine embroidery, stretch seams	100% nylon with special twist that creates stretch as you sew	70 denier/2
	Metallic	Shimmery foil-wrap bonded to thread core, available textured or smooth	Decorative stitching	Foil-wrapped core thread	40/2

Thread Type	Description	Uses	Fiber Content	Wt./Ply
Monofilament (Wonder Thread, Monofil)	Clear, lightweight, soft, single-strand nylon thread; appears invisible when used on right side of fabric; available clear or smoke-colored	Appliqué, couching, attaching sequins, soft rolled hems, joining lace strips, soft seam finishes, setting pockets, serging	100% nylon filament	.004 size
Serger, All-purpose	Comparable to all-purpose sewing machine thread, except serger thread is 2-ply	Finishing edges, seaming fabrics	Polyester core wrapped with fine cotton or 100% polyester	40/2
Serger, Decorative • Decor 6	Satiny soft thread with extra thickness because plies have minimal twist	Decorative serging, surface embellishment	100% viscose rayon filament	4-ply
• Glamour	Brilliant, glittery durable thread	Decorative serging, surface embellishment	65% viscose rayon, 35% metallic polyester	8-ply
• Pearl Cotton	Very lustrous Egyptian cotton thread	Decorative serging and stitching (size 30/2 is too heavy for stitching on conventional machine)	100% Egyptian cotton, double mercerized for sheen	30/2, 60/2
• Pearl Rayon	Strong, brilliant, colorfast rayon thread; available in solid or variegated colors	Decorative serging, surface embellishment	100% viscose rayon filament	40/2
Silk	Very lustrous	Embellishment, topstitching	100% silk	Varies
Sliver	Thin, flat, ribbonlike polyester film; infused with metal to make it brilliantly reflective	Decorative sewing, serging	Polyester film metalized with aluminum	1/100" thick
Woolly Nylon	Super-stretchy thread used as an edge finish or in seams that require stretch	Serging swimwear, lingerie, baby clothes; especially effective for rolled edges	Texturized (unspun) 100% nylon	NA

index

Nancy Zieman—businesswoman, home economist, and national sewing authority—is the producer and hostess of the popular show, "Sewing With Nancy," which appears exclusively on public television stations. The show, broadcast since September 1982, is the longest-airing sewing program on television. Nancy organizes each show in a how-to format, concentrating on step-by-step instructions.

Nancy also produces and hosts *Sewing With Nancy* videos. Each video contains three segments from her television program. Currently, there are 28 one-hour videos available to retailers, educators, libraries, and sewing groups.

In addition, Nancy is founder and president of Nancy's Notions, which publishes *Nancy's Notions Sewing Catalog*. This large catalog contains more than 4,000 products, including sewing books, notions, videos, and fabrics.

Nancy has written several books, including *Sew Easy Embellishments*, *501 Sewing Hints*, and *10•20•30 Minutes to Sew*. In each book, Nancy emphasizes efficient sewing techniques that produce professional results.

Nancy was named the 1988 Entrepreneurial Woman of the Year by the Wisconsin Women Entrepreneurs Association. In 1991, she also received the National 4-H Alumni Award. She is a member of the American Association of Family and Consumer Sciences and the American Home Sewing & Crafts Association.

Nancy lives in Beaver Dam, Wisconsin, with her husband and business partner, Rich, and their two sons, Ted and Tom.

For a complete line of sewing notions, turn to . . .

Nancy's Notions Sewing Catalog

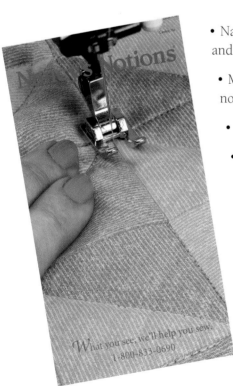

• Nancy Zieman's catalog for sewing, serging, and quilting enthusiasts.

• More than 4,000 products, including books, notions, videos, fabrics, and supplies!

• Value prices with built-in discounts!

• 100% satisfaction guaranteed!

For your free *Nancy's Notions Sewing Catalog*, send your name and address to:

Nancy's Notions
P.O. Box 683
Dept. 2318
Beaver Dam, Wisconsin 53916

Or call 1-800-833-0690.